DAS Hakpret ist ein alter fund/
Sein vrsprung aber ist nicht kund/
Doch meinen etlich für gewiß/
Das von der Harpfen es entspriß

Vnd von David sei erstlich gstifft/
Vnd wie solchs bezeigt Josephi Schrifft/
Der schreibt/ das David hab gar vil/
Erfunden newen Seitenspil/

Vnd außgetheilt inn die Leviten/
Einsonder Instrument ein jeden/
Deren eins soll das Hakpret sein:
Bei Fre. zen ist es sehr gemein: 6

In Glehrter schreibt: der Krieg sei hart:
Derhalben auch erfunden ward
Hart Messing Instrument zur sach/
Welchs noch die Leut vil härter mach/

Ja das die Pferd dahin kan pringen
Das sie zur schlacht gantz fräudig springen/
Josephus schreibt/ das Moses eben
Hat die Messin Trommet angeben/

Dargegen schreibet Plinius
Der Tirrhenisch König Priscus
Hab mit seim Volck die auf gebracht:
Im Krieg ward bessers nie erdacht. 8

So König Arggus dann entschlieff
Wie man mit einer Pfeiffen pfeiff:
Wie solt er nicht entschlaffen sein
Wann er solt hören heut allein

Ein Orgel mit so vilen stimmen/
Die man nicht kan genugsam rühmen/
Von wegen kunst vnd lieblichkeit/
Die also ist fürtrefflich heut/

Das Apollo (ders erstlich lehrt)
Sich müßt verkriechen/ wann ers hört/
Biewol er den Marsham schund
Der erst zwo Pfeiffen zammen bund. 4

Wiewol Minerve gar miß fällt
Die Pfeif/ weil sie den mund verstelt:
Sollman sich doch nicht ärgern lon/
Dann sie red wie ein Weib dar von:

Vnd vil mehr auf Poeten geben
Die solche Pfeif gar hoch erheben/
Weil sie inn der Natur bestehet
Vnd auch zu allen Spilen gehet.

Die Zwerchpfeif erstlich Midas macht
Nur auß Kranchbeinen vngeschlacht:
Die man darnach macht auß den Roren
Heut kan man sie zum schönsten boren. 5

EMANUEL WINTERNITZ

Musical Instruments

of the

Western World

PHOTOGRAPHS BY LILLY STUNZI

McGRAW-HILL BOOK COMPANY · NEW YORK · TORONTO

No parts of this work may be reproduced without the permission of the publisher.

All right herein are reserved.

Library of Congress Catalog Card Number 66–24889

71125

Printed and bound in West Germany.

The visual attraction of musical instruments has always been the concern of the craftsmen who built them, ever since the earliest phases of civilization; the frequent motto on Renaissance keyboard instruments, "pleasing to the eye and ear alike," is an appropriate formulation of this twofold ambition. While books abound that deal with the history of musical instruments, their function, and their importance for the study of the practice of performance, this visual appeal, curiously enough, has rarely been made the special topic of study or the main criterion for a selection of illustrations.

The word "pleasing" calls for an explanation. It is not supposed to mean what appears most beautiful to the author or to our time, but rather to the builder of the instrument and his contemporaries. The reader will therefore find instruments included which were regarded as appealing within their own environment, although today we may consider some of them as bizarre or overloaded with ornament or, on the other hand, too bare and simple.

A hundred examples are a pitifully small number for the representation of instruments from the late middle ages to our day; their selection was necessarily influenced by the predilection of the author. Thus, as always in such cases, some connoisseurs may miss their special favorites. Even more regrettable are the lacunae caused by the ravages of the last war. Still, I trust that the reader will find the present choice an organic and representative one, and will be stimulated to thought and fruitful comparisons by the variety of examples and the masterly photographs of Mrs. Lilly Stunzi.

Numerous public collections as well as private owners have kindly permitted me to have photographs made of musical instruments in their possession, for inclusion in this book: Metropolitan Museum of Art, New York; Sammlung alter Musikinstrumente, Kunsthistorisches Museum, and Gesellschaft der Musikfreunde, Vienna; Victoria and Albert Museum, London; Musée Instrumental du Conservatoire National de Musique, Paris; Germanisches Nationalmuseum, Nuremberg; Staatliche Musikinstrumentensammlung, Berlin; Musikinstrumentenmuseum, Karl Marx Universität, Leipzig; Städtische Instrumentensammlung, Munich; Bayerisches Nationalmuseum, Munich; Carl Claudius' Samling af Gamle Musikinstrumenter, Copenhagen; Musikhistorishe Museum, Copenhagen; National Museum, Copenhagen; Gemeentemuseum, The Hague; Yale University Collection of Musical Instruments, New Haven, Connecticut; British Museum, London; Ashmolean Museum, Oxford; Musée Instrumental du Conservatoire Royale de Musique, Brussels; Museo Civico, Bologna, Galleria Estense, Modena; the Principessa Henriette Barberini, Rome, the Honorable Irwin Untermyer, New York.

Of the many friends and colleagues who generously provided data concerning the instruments included, or filled lacunae in the available information, and helped Mrs. Stunzi in her work, I should like gratefully to mention: Dr. Alfred Berner, Mr. R. Bragard, Dr. Luisa Cervelli, Mme. H. Thibault de Chambure, Mr. Robert Conant, Dr. Henrik Glahn, Mr. A. W. Ligtvoet, Dr. Victor Luithlen, Mr. H. Macandrew, Dr. J. H. van der Meer, Dr. Winfried Schrammek, and Mr. Peter K. Thornton.

I received valuable aid from my colleagues at the Metropolitan Museum of Art: Miss Edith A. Standen, Mr. Carl Dauterman, Dr. Helmut Nickel, Mr. Joseph V. Noble, and Mr. James Parker, who helped in providing background material for the photographs and in many other ways. I am very much indebted to Dr. Olga Raggio, who made many valuable suggestions concerning special problems in the field of visual style and decoration. Another special measure of thanks goes to my assistant, Mrs. Eleanor Clark, without whose loving care, devoted help and unfailing memory, this book could not have been completed in so short a time.

Emanuel Winternitz

Form and Function

Musical instruments are strange and intriguing things. They are tools for producing organized sound – music. They have to comply with the immutable laws of acoustics. Bells require a certain material and thickness of their walls. Sounding boards of lutes and fiddles must be made of a certain wood so that the fibers can vibrate. Their strings have to be stopped by fingers or keys at certain points determined by mathematical ratios. Wind instruments have cylindrical or conical shapes. Their bore must have a certain width to produce the desired tones, and the finger holes are spaced according to certain proportions. Thus every instrument contains some elements which are shaped strictly according to the requirements of physical laws. Any deviation would thwart their purpose.

On the other hand, musical instruments are more than tools. They are objects not just to please the ear alone, but also the eye; they are decorative, and from the dawn of civilization they were often embellished with a wealth of decoration – carving, painting, gilding, and inlay were lavished upon them wherever their functional shape admitted. And often it was precisely their peculiar and strange functional form – the shape of curved horns and other serpentine wind instruments, or the complex sound boxes of spinets and harpsichords and other keyboard instruments – that invited the visual artist to contribute from his end and envelope the bizarre shapes with additional pictorial fantasy. An instrument like the violin, whose appealing beauty is largely the outcome of its functional purpose, is a remarkable exception.

One cannot, for instance, change the length of the neck of a violin, or its angle to the body, or the contour of the body, the curvature and thickness of its walls, or the placement and form of the bridge without affecting the balance of the whole. Here one could almost say that the shape of the whole instrument is the result of its function and of the acoustical requirements. The stunning beauty of a master violin is so perfect and logical that any accessory decoration such as carved reliefs or inlays or painting would hamper rather than enhance its visual appeal. In general one could say: the more complex the functional properties – that is, the compass, the dynamic range, and the ease and rapidity of playing – the greater the restrictions placed on the imagination of the instrument maker in his choice of a shape.

But often the function of an instrument permits some freedom, and then other shaping determinants come into play. One is the will to please the eye. "Pleasant to the ear as well as the eye" was a favorite motto painted on keyboard instruments of the Renaissance and early Baroque. As a rule the shape of an instrument is determined by both functional and extra-functional factors, and here the problem arises as to which parts are inflexible and cannot be altered by artistic imagination without impairing the function, and which parts invite the free play of decorative fantasy. Two outstanding showpieces may serve as examples: a) In the splendid harp made for the Farnese family, now in the collection of Princess Henriette Barberini (see Pl. 39), the front pillar, which plays no part in the generation of tone, is completely transformed into a profusely decorated tower of superimposed levels; the sound box, however, in the usual pyramidal shape, is entirely free of ornamental reliefs, since any decorative ballast would hamper the vibration of the sounding board and, to some extent, of the whole sound box. b) The famous cittern (cetra) commissioned in 1574 by the Archduke Ferdinand of Tyrol from Girolamo de Virchis of Brescia (see Pl. 8), now in the Vienna Kunsthistorisches Museum, shows the most elaborate sculptured decoration precisely at those points where the burden of added weight cannot impair free vibration – that is, at the shoulder and at the head of the neck, which is crowned with the figure of Lucretia stabbing herself. The soundboard as well as the back and the side walls of the body are free of carved decor, and only the sound hole has a beautiful painted and gilded rose similar to those found in contemporary lutes and guitars. Only in rare and exceptionally magnificent stringed instruments of the late Renaissance and the early Baroque does the carved decor invade the sound box, and even then rarely on the soundboard itself. One instrument of this sort is the beautiful violin of the seventeenth century, now in the Victoria and Albert Museum, in which the whole back is carved in flat relief with arabesques and ribbon knots. The back of another instrument, a violoncello bearing the Este family coat of arms, in the museum of Modena, is carved in deep relief to portray allegorical figures, angels, putti, and garlands (see Pl. 50). In such exceptional cases, the maker either had to take the trouble to achieve a workable compromise which would allow the necessary freedom of vibration despite the heavy decor, or simply had to content himself with producing an instrument pleasing to the eye rather than to the ear.

All these problems of the interaction of function and form naturally play a much lesser role in the realm of accessory decoration – that is, in those parts of the instrument where the ornamentation cannot conflict with the musical function. Cases in point are the painting, inlay, gilding, etc. of the exterior of European keyboard instruments and the stringed and woodwind instruments of many regions of the world: intricate carving of Near Eastern and European oliphants of the Middle Ages or of Renaissance and Baroque ivory horns and eighteenth century ivory recorders; or the molding of the metal bells of European slide trombones into the bizarre shape of dragon heads.

It is clear that the heavier types of ornament such as carving, stucco, or inlay can be tolerated only on the outer surfaces such as side walls, whereas painting can be applied even to soundboards, as for instance in Flemish virginals.

In the category of applied decoration must be mentioned the many and various devices or structures for suspending or supporting the sounding body of the instrument, and the cases protecting the instrument proper. Here belong structures, often with elaborately carved legs, carrying virginals, harpsichords, claviorgana, and pianofortes. Here also belong the profusely decorated protective outer wooden cases of Italian spinettini and cembali, usually made not by the instrument builder but by a special cabinet maker.

There are, of course, borderline cases between decor affecting the basic functional shape of the instrument and "applied" decoration, such as the unique *lira da braccio* made by Giovanni d'Andrea of Verona in 1511, whose soundboard is subtly curved to imitate a human torso (see Pl. 10).

In stringed instruments two areas in particular permit elaborate decoration. They are 1) the heads, or upper ends of the necks, which are often crowned with delicate carving such as the carved human heads on hurdy-gurdies and *viole da gamba* and pochettes, the traditional blindfolded Cupid on *viole d'amore*, the scroll on violins; and 2) the sound holes of lutes, bass lutes, guitars, citterns, and also of keyboard instruments such as Flemish virginals and Italian spinettini.

Instruments built for stage and other performances represent the most extreme case of the subordination of musical function to the demands of the eye. Among the most characteristic of this type are the instruments used in the Italian *sacre rappresentazioni*, *mascherate*, and *feste* of the fifteenth and sixteenth centuries. Many reports of such performances have survived: for instance, Vasari's detailed description of the *festa* given in Florence in 1565 on the occasion of the wedding of Francesco de' Medici and Johanna of Austria. Another rich source of information about theater instruments are the numerous preserved instructions given by stage directors to the theater workshops.

Many different kinds of mock instruments were built and used. Sometimes beautiful symbolical instruments were constructed simply to be held by allegorical personages, such as Apollo, the Muses, Orpheus, Hope, and Jealousy, while the sound was provided by real instruments hidden behind the stage. Frequently, actual instruments were adapted to the story, as for instance trumpets built in dragon shape or in the form of other monsters, to be blown by demons in Inferno scenes. Sometimes instruments were camouflaged with veils, other fabrics, cardboard, or various other materials according to their allegorical function on the stage. Thus, in an intermedium called "The Harmony of the Spheres" there were harps and lutes gilded to give them the semblance of *raggi celesti* or *Razzi di stelle*, and wind instruments fitted with shimmering artificial scales to appear as the serpents of Jealousy. In some instances the camouflage was only temporary; in one of the six intermedia inserted into Ambras's comedy *La Cofanaria*, Jealousy, Envy, Care, and Spite, when attacked by serpents, grabbed them and beat them with thorny sticks; but when Psyche burst into song these serpents shed their camouflage and were revealed as violins, and the sticks as fiddle bows, and in the hands of the four protagonists gave off the sweetest of harmonies. Frequently mythological personages were furnished with instruments *all' antica*—that is, constructed in the approximate shape of ancient Greek or Roman instruments, such as lyres or kitharas, yet playable in the modern, that is Renaissance, technique. At least one example of this type of grafting has survived. It is the lovely gold and blue bass lyre from the Obizzi collection, today in the collection of musical instruments of the Kunsthistorisches Museum in Vienna (see Pl. 16). In this unique instrument, the stylized silhouette of an ancient lyre is combined with the long neck and finger board of a bass lute or chitarrone, evidently for use in a mythological scene on the stage. Still another form of camouflage occurred in carnivals or masques, where dancers or people riding in the processions were occasionally dressed entirely as instruments. Among Leonardo's drawings for *feste*, for instance, is one of a rider on horseback disguised from head to toe as a bagpipe.

We have seen the interplay between two factors that shape an instrument: on the one hand, its function, and on the other, the ornamentation or decoration grafted onto this basic functional shape in order to please the eye. And it has been pointed out that in some cases the basic functional shape alone, such as that of the violin, can be of great beauty because of its interesting and well-proportioned design. Here it remains only to remark on some ornamentations in string, keyboard, wind, and percussion instruments which have not been discussed before.

In small string instruments, the usual methods of accessory decoration are carving, inlay, painting, and perforation of the sound boxes by sound roses, or sound holes. One should also mention the beauty bestowed on the sound boxes by the choice and combination of materials used. Lutes, guitars, chitarrones, and theorbos often have backs made by means of alternating staves of differing materials — woods of different color, or ivory and ebony. (See Plate 89.) Sometimes, even silver strips were inserted, as in lutes of the Renaissance. The correspondence of Isabella d'Este reveals that she commissioned

from Venice a lute with silver staves. And Giorgio Vasari, in his *Lives of the Painters*, reports of Leonardo da Vinci that he brought to Milan a lira made of silver in the shape of a horse skull. Show instruments were often made of other rare materials, certainly at the expense of their tonal beauty (or of any tone at all), such as the violin made of turtle shell for Empress Maria Theresia in 1749, in the Kunsthistorisches Museum, Vienna (see Pl. 84), and the seventeenth century guitar and violin made of Carrara marble, now in the Gallerie Estense in Modena (see Pl. 52, 53).

Various kinds of wood were chosen not only for their acoustical properties but for the design of their fibers. The vaguely irregular fiber patterns of the backs of violins made by the Cremonese dynasties have a special kind of fascination, and rightfully so. Patterns of one-piece backs, cut across the grain, have concentric oval curves, vaguely symmetrical; backs cut on the quarter consist of parallel bands running obliquely across, in alternating thickness and color; and two-piece backs excel by their often perfect symmetry.

The violin scrolls, changing from master to master, were beautifully and gracefully carved. Mention has been made of the viols, in which we frequently encounter carved heads representing human figures—an old tradition, as evidenced by countless instruments depicted in the drolleries ornamenting the margins of Books of Hours of the fourteenth and fifteenth centuries, or in the miniatures of the Cantigas de Santa Maria. Lutes, with their broad and characteristically bent necks, did not have carved heads. Hurdygurdies, however, although often made during the eighteenth century from the bodies of lutes and theorbos, frequently acquired a carved man's or woman's head at the top of their pegbox (see Pl. 73). Carving seldom invaded the area of the soundboard of an instrument, since the vibration could easily be impaired by uneven thickness.

A special and fascinating chapter in the evolution of European stringed instruments is presented by the sound holes, those windows in the sound boards that permit a communication between the air inside and outside of the sound box. They are of astounding variety and usually reflect the prevailing decorative style of the time. One line of evolution runs from primitive fiddles up to the violins of the great master builders. What appeared first as a round sound hole in the middle of the soundboard later became divided into two half-circles or half-moons, at the left and right of the strings. These simple patterns assumed the shape of C holes in viols, of intricate F holes in violins, or of the baroque flame holes frequent in *viole d'amore*. An even stranger pattern is found in the hook-shaped double holes in South German and Austrian barytons of the last decades of the eighteenth century.

The lute and the cittern retained their circular holes for centuries, and archlutes often had several circular holes. These sound holes were decorated with perforated stars or roses of various designs and material. Arabian lutes had and still have such roses made of bone or ivory. Those in European lutes were of wood, usually in Moresque or Gothic flamboyant design, and in the more precious lutes they were cut directly out of the soundboard rather than glued in. The famous lute makers competed in making intricate designs. The persistence of traditional sound hole patterns through generations is truly astonishing. Many lutes of the late Renaissance repeat in their roses geometrical ribbon "stars" which can be traced back to much earlier Arab architectural designs, such as those found in the window grills of Mosques.

Instruments are of aesthetic interest as furniture wherever they form an integral element of the interior. In Italy, princely palaces had keyboard instruments of considerable size for domestic music as early as the fifteenth century. To cite an outstanding example, the *studiolo* of Federigo da Montefeltre in his palace in Gubbio (now in the Metropolitan Museum of Art) shows among its life-size *trompe l'oeil* intarsias a magnificent positive organ. From the sixteenth century on, large keyboard instruments appear in burgher houses, especially, and for obvious reasons, in the North, where the home formed the center of family life and artistic activity, including performances of chamber or *haus* music. By the seventeenth century, many German homes had their *Klavier* or *Flügel* (both of these names indicating, at that time, large forms of the harpsichord), the Dutch *zitkamer* and English drawing rooms their virginals or wing-shaped harpsichords, and French salons their clavecins or épinettes. In the seventeenth and eighteenth centuries, the most substantial body of pictorial evidence of outstanding "musical furniture" is provided by the amplitude of Dutch interiors painted by Terborch, Metsu, Jan Steen, Molenaer, Pieter de Hooch, Vermeer, Frans van

Mieris, Gerard Dou, Kaspar Netscher, Verkolje, and others. A harpsichord, or more often a virginal, is almost standard equipment and frequently the decorative centerpiece of the *zitkamer*. From the end of the eighteenth century on, all these instruments were gradually replaced by the pianoforte in its many and rapidly changing shapes.

It goes without saying that the design of the sound boxes, protective cases, and legs reflected closely the prevailing style of furniture. Briefly, the following main types of furniture can be mentioned:

a) From the sixteenth century on, the strict, architectural form of the *cassone* became the model for regals and to some extent for the oblong boxes of virginals, though occasionally the shape of the credenza was borrowed. Usually the positive organs did not conceal their ranks of pipes in a protective case (see, for instance, one of the side wings of the Ghent altarpiece, Israel van Meckenem's engraving "The Organist and his Wife," and one of Hans Burgkmair's woodcuts for the "Weisskunig").

b) In the seventeenth century, the shapes of the *scrittojo* (writing cabinet) and of the *dressoire* became the accepted models for large chamber organs; their wooden cases were divided into a lower, wider section to house the bellows, and an upper, narrower section, usually equipped with opening doors, to house the ranks of pipes. In the sixteenth and seventeenth centuries, the visible frontal pipes were arranged either 1) symmetrically, with the longest pipe in the center, as in the South German organ, made in the first half of the seventeenth cen-

tury, illustrated in the catalogue of the Wilhelm Heyer Collection (No. 247); or 2) tapering from the large bass pipes on the left to the treble pipes on the right, as in the small German positive with painted side doors, of 1627, from the collection of the Elector Johann Georg I of Saxony, today in the Victoria and Albert Museum (see Pl. 38); or 3) in three groups symmetrically arranged in triptych fashion, as in the Italian positive bearing the coat of arms of the della Rovere family, made in the first half of the sixteenth century, in the Heyer collection (Cat. No. 241). (See Pl. 21.) Often the frontal space not filled by pipes was covered by carved and frequently gilded grillwork. One exceptional and unusually elaborate example among surviving chamber organs is the seventeenth century German Flügelschrank from the Ambras collection (Cat. No. 133/134) with its many little frontal drawers that completely hide the pipes.

The eighteenth century continued the same basic arrangement of the *dressoire* and credenza for chamber organs, but applied to the case the freely undulating and often bizarre contours and decor of the Rococo, one characteristic example being the Dutch positive from the middle of the century, with frontal pipes arranged in triptych fashion, in the Heyer Collection (Cat. No. 253).

In considering musical instruments as furniture, one should mention also certain instruments whose function is double, such as the jewel-box spinet *(Una spinetta a uso di forzerino di perle e rubini)* mentioned in the inventory of Lorenzo dei Medici of 1492, a combination of checkerboard, spinet, and regal made by Anton Meidling of Augsburg in 1587 (see Frontispiece), from the former collection of the Ambras castle and now in the Vienna Kunsthistorisches Museum; and also the fashionable nineteenth century sewing-box pianos with tray for needles, thread, and scissors placed on top of the soundboard.

Though they do not come under the category of *meuble*, one may mention other dual-function instruments, such as the many different kinds of boxes (*boite à musique*, *tabatière de musique*, *Spieldose*, and even a unique musical bustle which was given to Queen Victoria in 1887 and which was designed to play the national anthem when its wearer sat down) equipped with little hidden pin-barrel mechanisms acting on small pipes or steel combs, and the late eighteenth and early nineteenth century cane (walking-stick) instruments.

In Europe, the large keyboard instruments, because of their size and abundance of flat surfaces, lent themselves particularly well to pictorial decoration. Organs for church and home and certain types of harpsichords and pianofortes naturally invite painted or intarsia decoration, or reliefs in wood or stucco. In fact, the early instruments of this sort continued the fifteenth century tradition of the painted cassoni, and in later periods their decoration reflects trends in national styles as follows:

I. In instruments with harpsichord action, different traditions developed in the north and south: Flemish virginals and double virginals, whose oblong coffinlike cases were usually painted black and devoid of any exterior embellishment, were

Israhel van Meckenem: "The Organist and his Wife" (engraving).

13

lavishly decorated inside. Their soundboards were adorned with painted flowers and pewter sound-hole roses, the insides of the lids with landscapes or musical scenes, the inside of the front covers with Latin proverbs or musical mottoes, and large sections of the cases, in particular the frontboards, with wallpaper patterns. The most famous makers of such instruments were the Ruckers dynasty in Antwerp, founded by Hans Ruckers the Elder, who was admitted as Claversinbalmakerre to the Guild of St. Luke in 1575. Ruckers' instruments were widely exported to connoisseurs throughout Europe and in the Spanish colonies. Besides virginals, the Ruckers family and other Flemish builders made wing-shaped harpsichords (clavicembali); both kinds are depicted in the interiors of Vermeer, Terborch, etc. In the clavicembali, the frontboard and the inside of the top cover were usually covered by painting, while the outside of these instruments was just as inconspicuous as that of the virginals.

Unlike the Flemish harpsichords, Italian harpsichords of wing shape were usually constructed in two parts: the instrument itself, and a protective outer case from which it would be removed. This outer case was usually built by a special cabinet maker and was normally profusely decorated with paintings, both outside and on the inner side of the lid. The shape of those nonfunctional parts not strictly determined by acoustical requirements, notably the stand and the legs, followed the changing fashions of furniture style and reflected those furniture types closest to those parts in bulk and shape, such as the *cassoni*, tables, and the like. Only in the exuberant

Baroque era, less bound to any strict stylistic formulas than any other period, were keyboard instruments conceived as independent forms and constructed in eccentric and bizarre shapes. Perhaps the most outstanding of these showpieces is a harpsichord of fantastic shape in the Metropolitan Museum of Art (see Pl. 57). Another Italian harpsichord, of somewhat later date (last quarter of the seventeenth century), formerly in the Rospigliosi-Pallavicini collection, is supported by putti, musical trophies, and dolphins, and is decorated with paintings by Ludovico Gimignani.

The smaller instruments in Italy with harpsichord—that is, quill—action, namely the spinettine and ottavine of pentagonal or other polygonal shape, did not excel so much in painting as in the subtle combination of carving, of mother-of-pearl and wood intarsia, and of certosina work. In one of the finest and earliest specimens preserved, the spinettina which was made in 1540 in Venice for Eleonora, Duchess of Urbino (the daughter of that famous connoisseur of art and music and collector of art objects and musical instruments, Isabella d'Este) and which is now in the Metropolitan Museum of Art, even the jack rail is made of several layers of wood (see Pl. 20).

II. The pianoforte adopted decoration late, and then only gradually. The first piano, invented by Bartolommeo Cristofori in Florence in the early eighteenth century, was devoid of any ornamentation—its case and stand painted in uniform black. For some reason the profuse painting of harpsichords was not applied to its up-and-coming rival, the pianoforte. Even in Mozart's time, the only decorative feature of pianos worth speaking of was the careful veneer work of lid and side walls. A rapid change took place when the pianoforte began to replace the harpsichord and to become the bourgeois *meuble par excellence*. The Empire saw graceful square pianos *(Tafelklaviere)* lavishly painted, such as those decorated by Angelica Kaufmann and her imitators. Inlay, in precious wood and mother-of-pearl, and painting, as for instance gilt decoration with fruit and flower designs, were applied to the frontal surfaces. In the Biedermeier period, pianos with vertical soundboards became fashionable and were either in symmetrical shape ("lyre" or "pyramid" piano) or asymmetrical harp or wing shape ('Giraffe piano''), and the fronts of their soundboards were often protected by pleated silk screens. With the introduction of metal braces and frames for the reinforcement of the soundboards at the beginning of the nineteenth century, the pianoforte became a standardized issue of mass production and was thus no longer within the field of individual artistic imagination. Nonetheless, in the salons of Liszt's and Chopin's time in Paris, London, Vienna, Milan, and Berlin, when the piano formed the spiritual center of social gatherings, individually decorated showpieces appeared, sometimes completely covered by intricate marquetry, as, for example, the instruments decorated by master craftsmen such as George Henry Blake in London for the firm of Erard (see Pl. 100).

III. The history of the organ from its origin in Hellenistic Alexandria throughout some two thousand years of Mediterranean culture is beyond the scope of this book. Because of wars, fires, and the successive modernization of existing mech-anisms, few organs have survived intact from pre-Renaissance times. In the North, particularly in Germany, which was richer in large organs than Italy, many famous instruments were destroyed in the religious conflicts of the Reformation. Beginning with the fifteenth century many important churches had two organs, a large one in the nave or over the main portal, used for solo performances, and a smaller one in the choir for accompanying the singers and for playing during the service. Apart from large church organs conceived as part of the architecture, several types of free-standing organs developed, chiefly for secular use:

"Positives," or chamber organs; and still smaller "portatives," used at home, at court events, and often carried on cars in processions (Burgkmair, Dürer, etc.).

Organetti, even smaller, which were carried by a leather strap around the neck of the player.

The regal, which, placed on a table, contained one set of short reed pipes operated by two rectangular bellows.

One important aesthetic problem posed by church as well as chamber organs was that of symmetry, since the natural arrangement of pipes, starting with the longer and larger bass pipes and ending with the smaller and shorter treble pipes, would have been in a descending diagonal line. A reconciliation of the acoustical and visual requirement was achieved in the symmetrical deployment of the pipes. This problem naturally affected only the front pipes, known as the "prospect," which concealed other ranks behind. One frequent solution was a pyramidal arrangement, with the longest pipe in the center; another was the division of the prospect into three compartments in tryptich fashion, with the longer pipes in the middle compartment, as in the beautiful organ in San Giovanni in Laterano, Rome (see Pl. 29). Large church organs had even more compartments, from five to seven, each housing a special rank of pipes. The easiest solution for a pleasingly symmetrical prospect was, of course, in the use of "blind" or "mute" pipes, creating a false decorative front.

The climax of organ decoration was reached during the Baroque period in Catholic countries, especially in Spain, and under the banners of the Counter Reformation in Bavaria. The organ became the great showpiece of the church, an integral part of the colorful sculptured, stuccoed, and painted church interior, outstanding not only in size but in visual splendor (see Pl. 85). Its visible front pipes were gilded, painted, or embossed in ornamental patterns, or hidden behind large pyramids of "mute" pipes. Large wooden fronts teeming with angels, saints, putti, and decorative vases encased the pipe compartments of the organ.

The important treatises on organ construction in the Baroque period rarely mention the visual, decorative aspects. However, Jakob Adlung's *Musica Mechanica Organoedi* (Berlin, 1768) includes an interesting section devoted "to the eye rather than to the ear": "If an organ is rightly constructed, it serves as special adornment of the house of the Lord." Among the problems discussed by Adlung are: the correct placement of the instrument ("at which point of the compass, and how high or low, so that the right light may fall upon it"); the require-

ments of "Eurythmie" for symmetrical appearance; the spatial grouping of the pipes, the use of mute pipes "for filling optical gaps" and, for the same purpose, the use of carved ornaments such as "flames, pyramids, roses, musical instruments, statues, the sun, stars, scrolls . . ."

The detailed history of the church organ as an integral aesthetic element of the church interior, as well as of the evolution of rood lofts for organs, belongs largely within the history of church architecture.

Regals and organetti, because of their shape and generally small size, offered only limited surfaces for decoration, but the two pillars that flank the ranks of pipes of positives, even in their smaller models made to be placed on tables, invited carving and inlay. These pillars were also often crowned by carved figures, as for instance on the charming instrument depicted in one of the famous Unicorn Tapestries, circa 1500, now in the Cluny Museum in Paris.

The larger positives, or chamber organs, placed on the ground were an important factor in house music of the Renaissance, especially north of the Alps. They were a common piece of furniture used at home alongside the harpsichord and the clavichord. These chamber organs, as well as small church organs, were nearly always protected by wooden cases which, just like the lids and side walls of virginals and clavicembali, offered ample surface space not only for painted ornamentation, but even for good-sized paintings. Such paintings on the doors of organ cases, on the inner sides of virginal lids, and on both sides of harpsichord lids were standard practice in the

Renaissance and Baroque eras, and, following the tradition of *cassone* painting, were often commissioned from great masters. According to Vasari (Vita di Pontormo), Bronzino painted the case of a harpsichord for Guidobaldo, the Duke of Urbino; and in the Hermitage Museum there is an exquisite painting, attributed to both Correggio and Bronzino, of the contest between Apollo and Marsyas. Its unusual form, originally wing-shaped but later expanded into a rectangle, indicates that it was intended for the decoration of a harpsichord lid. Most of these decorative paintings were naturally related to music. For organ cases, sacred subjects were preferred, such as King David, Santa Cecilia, angel concerts, etc. The keyboard instruments for secular use admitted as well representations of musical parties, pastoral scenes, and above all mythological subjects such as Parnassus, the Muses (alone or with Apollo), the contests of Apollo with Pan and with Marsyas, and Orpheus and Arion. Sometimes amusing combinations occurred: for instance, on the inside of the front section of the lid, which could be opened separately at formal occasions, appeared an angel concert, while the rear section displayed a reclining Venus, who evidently graced less serious musical parties.

The most elaborate instructions written during the High Renaissance for the pictorial decoration of keyboard instruments are to be found in the *Trattato dell' Arte della pittura, scultura ed architettura* (1584) by Giovanni Paolo Lomazzo. For the ornamentation of church organs he recommends a long list of sacred topics, all of which should have some inner relation to music, thus ruling out such scenes as the conver- sion of Saint Paul, the Annunciation, battle scenes, sacrifices, and miracles. The secular instruments, those used at court and private homes, were to be decorated with mythological or allegorical subjects or representations of the nine choirs of heavenly musicians. Each choir should be devoted to one type of instrument and should contain portraits of the three most ex- cellent musicians associated with it. The twenty-seven famous musicians he suggests include, for instance, Leonardo da Vinci, who was renowned for his virtuosity on the *lira da braccio*.

There is yet one more area of keyboard instruments which invited decorative fantasy; the sound holes (usually one, though sometimes two) which perforated the soundboards of virginals and clavicembali. An inexhaustible wealth of patterns was lavished on these small circular openings. Different national traditions existed for various instruments. Flemish virginals, for instance, usually had roses of pewter representing an alle- gorical figure such as Pan or an angel, flanked by the initials of the instrument maker; while Italian clavicembali or spinetti frequently had roses made of extremely thin wood carved in geometrical patterns (see Pl. 20c, spinetta of Eleonora d'Este) and often three-dimensional "sunken roses" consisting of several layers of wood or parchment.

Even simple shapes like that of recorders, consisting of one solid tube, are sometimes elaborately carved, especially in instruments made of ivory (see Pl. 62). Such carving often takes the form of leaf decoration, or *mascheroni*; or the whole head of the recorder is made to look like that of a dragon, with the jaws forming the square mouth of the instrument. In

transverse flutes and in reed instruments, which are made of several joints, such carving is out of the question: but the proportions between the single joints (usually three or four) have their own charm, which is frequently enhanced – most beautifully in English, French, and German instruments of the Baroque – by a rich profile and rings of bone or ivory that mark the joints between the several sections (see Pl. 63). Recorders of the eighteenth century also often had bone or ivory terminal pieces which, together with the joints, make an impressive contrast to the dark main tube. Decorative painting on flutes or other woodwinds is rare, since it would be apt to wear off with handling. However there were porcelain flutes, especially transverse flutes, which were often richly decorated and formed a beautiful addition to the other contemporary Sèvres and Meissen products (see Pl. 77).

The richer and more complex the key mechanism became, especially under the impact of Gordon's and Boehm's inventions for the flute, the less room there was for decoration; the same became true of all woodwinds.

Brass instruments already attract the eye by the beautiful shape and proportions of their coils, and any showcase combining such instruments from the time of the Renaissance on would display an interesting variety of coiling, from the S-shaped trumpets of the early Renaissance, to those of later times with parallel coiling, to the horns antedating the invention of valves, showing all kinds of spiral coils. One would perhaps think that the beautifully shining and regular surface of a metal tube would neither need nor admit any accessory decoration, but this is not so. Trumpets from the time of the Middle Ages were the aristocrats among musical instruments. Only monarchs and great nobles were privileged to use them as sign and symbol of their rank. They were associated with certain ceremonial and military functions. As military instruments they were the monopoly of the highest-ranking branch, the cavalry. The trumpet retained this aristocratic and military character and symbolism in the Baroque period, for instance in Handel's operas and oratorios; and later in the Classical Viennese period of music, in works such as the masses and symphonies of Haydn; and even up to our time.

Trumpets were often made of silver, both for the sake of appearance and to provide a certain timbre, and were decorated with the greatest elegance. The long tube was elaborately reinforced by ferrules, sleeves, and bosses, and all these elements were elaborately engraved or chased with floral designs or other ornaments. Also, the rim of the bell or the whole bell branch was decorated by elaborate molding or engraving. Often the best silversmiths and armorers were engaged for this type of work. Especially famous were the trumpets made by instrument makers in Nuremberg, for instance those by the family of Schnitzer in the sixteenth century, particularly Anton Schnitzer, and by their successors in the seventeenth century, for example Michael Nagel. Some glorious examples of silver trumpets by these makers are now in the collection of the Kunsthistorisches Museum in Vienna (see Pl. 27.)

Similar decoration was naturally bestowed on the larger cousin of the trumpet, the slide trombone. The picturesque effect of

this instrument was even more enhanced by the addition of customary heraldic banners, pennants, cords, and tassels (see Pl. 41 and 59).

Another frequent and characteristic ornamentation of larger brass instruments was the transformation of the bell into a dragon or serpent's head. Such frightening reptile heads had already occurred in theatrical and fantastic instruments both in the open processions of Renaissance feasts and in the intermedia, those Renaissance forerunners of opera. Military wind bands used the same decoration for trombones and later around 1800 for bass horns, often with the addition of a trembling tongue and imitation of the scales of a serpent skin (see Pl. 95, 94). Sometimes the animal shape went even further and engulfed the whole instrument. In Far Eastern instruments this was no rarity; we may recall the Indian peacock lute or the Chinese fish (a wooden slit drum used in religious ceremonies). But in the Occident I know of only one instrument of this type, the Tartölten—shawms, whose tubes consisting of many closely coiled spirals were hidden inside a dragon-shaped body. The dragon's tail was formed of a metal tube furnished with a double reed while the lower end of the instrument was formed by the open mouth of the dragon, with a flexible tongue between the jaws. Only one set of five such instruments—bass, two altos, two descant—have survived as a unique treasure in the Vienna Kunsthistorisches Museum (see Pl. 17).

Elaborately decorated metal mountings occurred not only in metal instruments but also as ornamentation of wooden or ivory instruments such as the Cornetti (*Zinken*)—straight or curved conical tubes which combined the finger holes of a woodwind instrument with the mouthcup of a "brass" instrument (see Pl. 62).

A special case of impressive coiling is found in the Scandinavian *Lur*, dating back to the Bronze Age—a long bronze horn curved in the shape of a contorted S, with a typical horn mouthpiece at one end and a flat ornamental disc at the other (see Pl. 2).

The category of idiophones comprises such a variety of forms and functions that general observations about their decorative values are hardly possible. Also, many of the percussion instruments such as triangles, jew's harps, lithophones, xylophones, and metallophones are purely functional, with no pretensions as to eye appeal. In the present book, devoted predominantly to the visual beauty of instruments, we will therefore single out only a few examples.

Among rattles we find some which have special decoration in line with their religious and folk customs, as for instance the rattles used to "break the bones of Judas" on Good Friday and the medieval crecelle used to replace the sound of church bells during the week before Easter, when the bells supposedly "travelled to Rome" (see Pl. 5).

The surface decoration of bells of course followed the prevailing artistic styles of the period. Their main shape, however, was standardized: large church bells existed as early as the eleventh century and were usually cast in the shape of beehives, a form that was replaced in the thirteenth century by the modern tulip shape.

Historical Aspects

Among the most important factors that influence the evolution of musical instruments are, on one hand, the prevailing musical style of a period and, on the other hand, the status of technology. Both of these factors are in a perpetual state of flux, and it is not possible to formulate general rules as to their interaction. Looking back at the history of instrumental music since prehistoric time, one finds numerous cases in which the invention of a new tool or a decisive technical improvement of a pre-existing tool kindled the imagination of the instrument maker and thus led to a transformation of the music itself. On the other hand, examples can be mentioned where the stimulus for change started with the musician rather than the instrument maker. In such cases, the imagination of the composer or player sought for new mechanical contrivances for producing sounds, and the instrument maker then produced the needed tool "to measure," as it were. When Richard Wagner desired a special solemn timbre for certain orchestral passages in his *Ring*, he demanded and received from the instrument maker a new kind of brass instrument, the "Wagner tuba." It so happens that two of the most popular instruments of our day, the pianoforte and the violin, represent different extremes. When Bartolommeo Cristofori invented the pianoforte he gave to his era, greedy for new dynamic effects, the appropriate tool in the form of a keyboard instrument with hammer mechanism to permit gradual increase or decrease of tone volume through the modification of finger pressure exerted upon the keys. The violin, however, existed a considerable time before its inherent dynamic and tonal resources were ex-ploited by Vivaldi, and later, in an unforeseeable way, through the invention of a supplementary tool, the Tourte bow.

Sometimes it is another factor, the visual appeal of the shape, that contributes to the invention or improvement of an instrument. Here again, one exemplary case in point is the violin. Its "invention" must, in fact, have been due to the aesthetic sensitivity of unknown master craftsmen in the early sixteenth century who, searching for a "perfect" form—that is, for an organic and unified whole—brought about the crystallization of older types and forms of the fiddle into a balanced union of undulating contours and gracefully molded planes.

At the same time, a beautiful and standardized shape may resist functional changes to a nearly absurd degree. This is the case with the shape of the ancient classical lyre and cythara, with their two arms supporting a yoke to which were attached the "open" strings. Long after its playing technique had been superseded by the addition of a finger board or neck, the arms survived in more or less atrophied form, devoid of practical function. What is even more striking is that in periods of renascences of Antiquity, such as the Carolingian era, the Quattro- and Cinquecento, and the French Empire, arms were added to instruments with central finger boards purely to give them the appearance of the kithara or lyre.

The frequent assumption that the invention of new instruments can be attributed exclusively either to technological progress or to new musical ideas has often led to an oversimplified interpretation of musical history. Actually, generalizations are not possible and each case has to be investigated on its own

merits. It is interesting that some mechanical devices used for producing sound, though comparatively simple, were not applied to musical instruments until centuries after their invention, at a point when musical thought was ready to employ them. Valves for brass instruments, to mention one example, were not invented until around 1830, but their construction would have presented no major difficulty to the metal craftsmen of Augustean Rome, who devised the subtle metal rings, or collars, which could be revolved to shut off or diminish the diameter of the finger holes of the Roman double oboe (aulos or tibia).

Each thoughtful observer of a musical instrument of the past will naturally try to relate it to the music of its time, and try to understand it as the best, or at least typical, tool for executing the kind of music that was fashionable then. Yet this mental procedure, this interpretation of an object to determine what it could give to its time and environment, and what the performers and composers of its time demanded from it, is not an easy task. Music, like any other art, constantly changes its character throughout the centuries, sometimes slowly and almost imperceptibly, and sometimes violently, in sudden revolutions against the established style. The instrumentaria of the past—of the early and late Medieval ones, of the Renaissance and Baroque orchestras, and of the Romantic era—were different in many regards because they served different purposes, different textures of music, and different predilections for tone color. But if there was an evolution, it should not be called progress. Progress, that is, actual improvement, exists only in the realm of technology, where better solutions for certain mechanical problems are found through the inventions of practical devices that solve mechanical problems better than had been done before. Keys added to wind instruments made them more easily playable and expanded their range of tones. The invention of keyboard instruments, the organ, clavichord, harpsichord, and pianoforte, made possible a wealth of polyphony and harmony not hitherto available. The invention of the valve mechanism made all the tones of the chromatic scale easily available on brass instruments. Of comparable importance was Erard's invention of the double-action harp, and devices for rapid retuning of modern kettledrums. They all are improvements in the strict sense of the word, solving some technical problems better than had been done before.

But one cannot speak of improvement with regard to the basic kinds of instruments themselves. Stringed and wind instruments, as they appear successively in the mainstream of Occidental music, are not better or worse—they are different. The four-stringed violin of the eighteenth century is not better than a six-stringed *viola da gamba* of the seventeenth century; they serve different musical purposes. The violin, with its greater tension of strings and bow hair, could play louder than the soft-tensioned, thin-stringed viol, but it had to pay a price— it lost some of the polyphonic possibilities inherent in the viol, which permitted the bow to touch three strings simultaneously. As a matter of fact, the violin was objected to and maligned for its ignoble shrieking when it first appeared. And more than a century after its origin, it was censured by a connoisseur of such stature as Marin Mersenne, who, in his *Harmonie Universelle*, 1636, says of violins: "... *non peut les appeller imitateurs de la viole ... mais ils ne lèsgallent pas, car le violon a trop de rudesse, d'autant que l'on est contraint de le monter de trop grosses chords.*" Likewise the silver flute of the modern orchestra was criticized for having abandoned the velvety wooden tone of its predecessor. The tone of the cornetto (zink) was praised by Father Mersenne in his *Harmonie Universelle* and compared to a ray of sunshine cutting through the dark clouds, but ridiculed by Berlioz in his *Traité de l'Instrumentation* (1843), who compared it to the horrible shrieks heard at the bloody sacrifices of the Druids.

In short, every period of music had its ideal of sound and tone color. In former times musicians were often intolerant towards the past, or even ignorant of it. If earlier masterworks were performed at all, they were adapted with no inhibitions to contemporary notions of good timbre; a remarkable case in point is Mozart's reorchestration of Handel's *Messiah*. It is only in our own eclectic time that we have learned to revive, or rather to reconstruct, the aesthetic atmosphere of earlier periods of music and apply this knowledge to the performance of masterworks of the past.

It is with this in mind that the student of musical instruments should approach even a single instrument, and revive the aesthetic intentions of its time. Lack of space here forbids giving more than the briefest outline of the history of instruments, even for the span of time from which our pictorial examples are taken.

The Middle Ages knew a great variety of instruments of all kinds. While the heritage of Greek-Roman civilization was drowned in the continuous waves of the great migration from the northeast, Celtic civilization left its lasting impact through the wandering of vagrant monks and minstrels with harps and lyres. Later, it was the Orient, especially the impact of Moslem culture, that decisively enriched the occidental instrumentarium through many forms such as lutes, mandole, guitars, bowed fiddles, psalteries, trumpets, kettledrums, reed pipes, and fipple flutes. Moorish Spain and southern Italy functioned as the main entrance gates. The Crusades contributed to the cultural exchange; and even in the eighteenth century the Turkish invasions left their mark in the military bands of the central European armies.

Many life-sized sculptures of musical instruments have survived in the tympana of Romanesque cathedrals, where we find interesting vielles and other stringed instruments in the hands of the twenty-four Apocalyptic Elders. A major source of our knowledge of Medieval instruments are the Carolingian illuminated manuscripts, above all the Utrecht Psalter with its portrayal of musicians surrounding the psalmist; and later a long row of psalteries such as the Stuttgart, the Cantigas de Santa Maria, the Manesse Handschrift, the Queen Mary and Luttrell Psalters, and the fifteenth-century Books of Hours whose margins are peopled by demons, jugglers, half-animals, and other jolly creatures, often engaged in music, plucking, bowing, blowing, and striking bells and chimes of various kinds. But pitifully few instruments have survived to our day. Two remarkable exceptions are two plucked instruments of boxwood which, probably because of their exceptionally rich carving, must have early become parts of princely collections and thus managed to escape decay and worms. One is an English gittern, formerly owned by the Earl of Warwick, which has recently come to the British Museum (see Pl. 3). This instrument is remarkable for the lavish carving on its side wall representing leaves, animals, and archers. The other is a small stringed instrument in the collection of the Hon. Irwin Untermyer in New York (formerly in the Figdor Collection, Vienna), (see Pl. 4), which has beautiful carvings on its back, neck, and head, showing a falconer and his sweetheart, a cupid, a stag, and other figures relating to the hunt; on its head is a maiden playing a lute.

After the rise of vocal polyphony, instruments were combined into larger groups, to reinforce the vocal parts or to perform an instrumental polyphony. At the same time a desire for a great variety of tone colors resulted in a wealth of timbres never again achieved in the history of music, not even in the modern standardized symphony orchestra. The most characteristic aspect of Renaissance instruments was their grouping into families, with each family—winds as well as strings—comprising many members of different sizes, each of small compass, corresponding to a range of the human voice, and going from small high-treble instruments to gigantic double basses. There was a bass viol seven and a half feet long and a *Gross Bass-Pommer* ten feet long. A family of recorders, for instance, was made up of eight sizes and, when used as a choir, included no

less than twenty-one instruments—a homogeneous group, perhaps best compared with one of the registers of an organ, consisting of a great number of pipes of the same timbre. The double reeds alone had many families, such as the *bassanelli*, *Rauschpfeifen*, *Schreierpfeifen*, *cromorni*, and *sordoni*, names already long forgotton by the time of Johann Sebastian Bach. In addition to these choirs of instruments in which polyphony was created by the cooperation of several single-voiced instruments, there were also solo instruments which could produce polyphony unaided, such as the keyboard instruments: organ, regal, harpsichord, clavichord, and, to a lesser extent, the many-stringed lutes, viols, and *lire da braccio* and *da gamba*. Praetorius, who in his *Organographia* at the beginning of the Thirty Years War in 1618 summed up the late Renaissance instrumental practice, enumerates no less than eleven families of woodwind instruments (transverse flutes, recorders, *bassanelli*, *sordunen*, rackets, bassoons, *Schreierpfeifen*, *Rauschpfeifen*, Krummhorns, shawms, and cornemuses) of which, for instance, the family of recorders had eight sizes. There were also trombones, trumpets, and cornettos, and among the many string instruments, whole families of violins, viols, and a number of other stringed instruments including the *lire da braccio* and the keyboard instruments, which were not built in families.

At this point we should say a few words on the invention of the keyboard and the evolution of keyboard instruments, which today play such a dominant role in church and home and concert hall.

 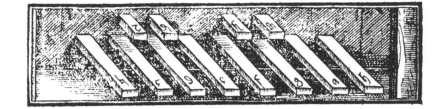

In the push-button society we live in today, the keyboard, be it on a typewriter, an IBM machine, or a piano, has become such an indispensable part of our mechanized world that it is taken for granted. However, for the historian and student of music, it may not be without interest to examine the nature and origin of this significant development in musical history. One may define a keyboard as a set of levers that serve as an extension of the player's fingers: when he depresses them they enable him to control distant points in the mechanism of his instrument. So simple is the keyboard in principle that one cannot but wonder why it was not invented by ancient peoples with highly developed technology, such as the Egyptians, the Greeks, and the Romans. Aristotle mentions cogwheel mechanisms, the Egyptians of Ptolemaic times pumped water by machinery, and Vitruvius describes mechanical gadgets to measure the mileage of the horse-drawn Roman "taxis" and, in the field of music, an elaborate hydraulic organ. Why then was the keyboard not invented until the Middle Ages?

Perhaps the answer lies in the interaction between musical thought and the tools of music; the realm of matter functions, as it were, as a floodgate for the stream of ideas. The structure of ancient Greek music, Gregorian and Byzantine chant, and, later still, the music of the twelfth-century troubadours and *trouvères* was predominantly monophonic: it consisted of a single melodic line with no accompaniment or only a simple one. As long as this musical structure prevailed, there was no need for a mechanism that could produce several simultaneous voices – in other words, polyphony. Only after the rise of polyphony in the Occident could people conceive of an instrument that would bring into the reach of one player the voices or melodic strands produced by several singers or players. Only after the final victory of this style were keyboards in their modern sense – that is, with rapid control of numerous simultaneous tones – constructed.

The origin of the modern keyboard dates back to the Middle Ages. Among its antecedents are the levers used in the monochord, the organistrum, and the early pipe organ. Medieval monks used the monochord to determine the precise dependence of the musical intervals upon certain arithmetical ratios of length of string. It was an oblong wooden box with one string, later several, stretched over its sounding board. The strings were stopped by movable bridges that had to be raised or lowered by the player's hands. Eventually these bridges were replaced by more practical and rapidly responding levers so pivoted that when the front of the lever was depressed by the player's finger, the rear part was raised toward the string. Though there are no treatises to substantiate this, it would seem logical to assume that this early key mechanism played an important role in the development of the clavichord, which as late as the Renaissance was still called *monocordium* or *manicordo*. The fifteenth-century clavichord that is depicted in the intarsias of the study of Federigo da Montefeltro in his palace at Urbino is so large and complex that it must be considered the fruit of an already lengthy evolution.

Another and more primitive key mechanism is found in the Medieval organistrum, frequently represented among the instru-

ments played, as described above, by the twenty-four Apocalyptic Elders in the tympana of Romanesque churches, as at Moissac and Santiago de Compostela. Its strings, stretched over a long, rectangular sound box, were vibrated by a wheel turned by a crank at the end of the instrument. One player turned the crank while the other manipulated with both hands a set of stopping rods that raised small bridges placed beneath the strings. The handles of the rods were on the upper side of the instrument as it lay across the laps of both players, and therefore the rods could not fall away from the strings of their own weight. The organistrum was the ancestor of the hurdy-gurdy (*vielle à roue* or "fiddle with a wheel"), which is still played by French peasants. Just when it was improved we do not know, but in frescoes of the school of Giotto the modern hurdy-gurdy keyboard is clearly shown. The stopping rods are now on the lower side and thus fall back automatically; a single player can push them with one hand while turning the crank with the other.

The pipe organ acquired a keyboard relatively late. Giant instruments like the tenth-century organ in the monastery at Winchester, with no less than four hundred pipes and twenty-six bellows pumped by seventy men, had no keyboards in the modern sense, but rather a row of slides called *linguae*, or "tongues." These were wooden boards that projected from the wind chest and could be pulled out to open the channels leading from the wind chest to all the pipes of the same pitch. They were cumbersome and ran in wooden grooves. One can imagine what the damp English climate did to them—and also what muscle power was demanded of the player, who could not have manipulated them in rapid succession. No wonder a smoother method of operation was sought. The solution was found in the eleventh century when the tongues were replaced by wooden levers that could be depressed vertically to open valves inside the wind chest and allow the compressed air to flow into the pipes. Clumsy as these primitive keys must have been, they were an important step in the gradual evolution of the keyboard that, after many centuries of development, culminated in the keys of the modern organ, which at the lightest touch instantaneously release the sound of many hundreds of pipes. An early landmark in this evolution was the organ in the cathedral of Magdeburg at the end of the eleventh century: it had a fully developed keyboard of sixteen notes. Early keyboards were sometimes inside the wind chest and therefore are not visible in many representations found in paintings and sculpture. What we often see are push-buttons similar to those of a modern accordion; when they were pushed they depressed the front ends of the hidden keys. It is not until the Renaissance that one finds the question of the origin of the keyboard posed in musical treatises, with answers based rather on guesswork than on historical evidence. Vincenzo Galilei, the father of the famous astronomer, wrote an ingenious book, *Dialogo della musica antica e della moderna* (Florence, 1581), in which he relates the invention of the harpsichord—which he does not call by the later Italian term *clavicembalum* ("cymbalum with keys"), but rather *harpicordo*—"to the harp." "Although Italian musicians claim it as their invention, it had its origin in the harp, and is really nothing but a horizontal harp with keys added," he says, pointing as proof to the similarity in name and shape and in the number, disposition, and material of the strings.

Of all the keyboard instruments, the clavichord is the simplest in construction and probably the oldest. When the finger depresses the key, a little brass plate called the tangent, attached to the rear part of the key, not only strikes the string to make it vibrate, but also divides it into two parts, one of which is deadened by a damping cloth. In the earlier, "fretted" clavichord, one string could be struck at different times by more than one tangent, thereby producing more than one tone. It was not until the eighteenth century that the fretted clavichord was gradually replaced by the unfretted type, which had a different string for each key. Though the tone of the clavichord is extremely soft, the volume can be modified by finger pressure, an effect not possible at the harpsichord.

In instruments of the harpsichord family the strings are plucked by quills or leather plectra, which disengage immediately after contact with the string. Thus tone volume cannot be modified by finger pressure but only by adding more strings — that is, by bringing one or more sets of strings into play by means of the stops.

It has become a common convention among historians of music to use the convenient date of 1600 as the beginning of the Baroque era. Two of the great stars of Renaissance polyphony, Palestrina and Orlando Lasso, had disappeared; and at about the same time there began a decisive turn from the old, venerable, polyphonic tradition towards a new ideal of expressiveness — monody, a leading melody against a neutral background harmony. In musical notation the chords of this background harmony were condensed by an ingenious shorthand device, the thorough bass.

The texture of the various new Baroque phenomena — opera, oratorio, cantata, and the instrumental concerto — was largely based on this new principle of distinction between a protagonist melody and a background harmony. The new approach to musical texture became apparent with surprising swiftness, but if we compare this revolution in musical style with the alteration of its technical tools — the instruments — we cannot find, by any means, so sharp a change.

Seen beside the Renaissance heritage, the Baroque orchestra appears impoverished in number and kind. Only gradually, almost imperceptibly, did the orchestra of the Baroque period evolve from the enormous instrumentarium of the Renaissance. A process of selection and standardization began, which can best be interpreted as a survival of the fittest or of those instruments which best served either as soloists or as vehicles of background harmony. Thus the large families of reed instruments gradually fell into oblivion. Of the strings, those families survived which best met the new stylistic requirements by forming the instrumental background chorus — which was to become the *tutti* in the Baroque concerto — and the accompanying orchestra in opera. These survivors were the families of the violins and the viols. On the other hand there was a need for solo instruments with a wider compass and greater dynamic

and tonal flexibility. Out of the various types of Renaissance double-reed instruments with doubled tubes, such as the kortholts, the *sordoni*, dolcians, *doppioni*, and *fagotti*, evolved the versatile Baroque bassoon, furnished with keys and made in separate joints, as we know it in Johann Sebastian Bach's orchestra. Similarily, out of the family of Renaissance shawms developed the keyed and jointed oboe of the eighteenth-century orchestra, with its lower-pitched sisters the *oboe d'amore*, the *oboe da caccia*, and the English horn. The shawm family itself, however, continued to live on in improved and refined form far into the seventeenth century; at its peak it consisted of seven sizes ranging in length from one to ten feet. Likewise, the family of recorders, consisting of eight sizes in Praetorius's time, continued throughout the seventeenth century, although by that time it was shrinking slowly to five sizes, of which there are examples of the jointed type, with its typical Baroque contour, and of ivory recorders, exquisitely carved and of a beautiful, velvety tone.

Flauto in the scores of Alessandro Scarlatti, Lully, Bach, and Handel still meant the recorder, not the transverse flute. The latter was one of the few woodwind instruments that existed in only three sizes in the Renaissance orchestra. In its new conical one-keyed form it was to become one of the most expressive and fashionable solo instruments of the eighteenth century, as we know from the amount of music written for it and from numerous treatises written on it from the days of Louis Hotteterre to those of Quantz, the teacher of Frederick the Great, who was a devoted player of the *traversière* (see Pl. 63).

The transformation of the brass instruments in the Baroque period took place in so many different ways in various countries that it cannot be readily summarized. In general, the majestic choir of trombones was inherited unchanged from the Renaissance. The trumpet also persisted, retaining its different registers — the extremely difficult and virtuoso *Clarino* and the medium *Principale* register. Germany, especially Nuremberg, still retained its importance as the center for making these instruments.

The only true newcomer to the brass orchestra of the Baroque period grew out of the rather primitive hunting horn by a lengthening of its tube and a narrowing of its bore; it was the "lovely-pompous waldhorn," as Mattheson in 1713 called it, "better and rounder in tone than the deafening and shrieking trumpet."

Another Renaissance wind instrument, the cornetto, or zink, a wooden or ivory tube with finger holes and a cup-shaped mouthpiece, persisted in general use in its various forms, as *diritto*, *curvo*, *torto*, and *muto*, and in various sizes until the end of the seventeenth century (see Pl. 62), when it was replaced by the modernized woodwinds in the Baroque orchestra, the one-keyed transverse flute, the two-keyed oboe, and the three-keyed bassoon. The cornetto still occurs in Bach cantatas and in some of Gluck's scores. The treble zink, which was once so famous for its almost-human voice and coloratura technique, succumbed to the solo violin.

Turning to the stringed instruments, and first to the bowed ones, long before 1600 two distinct families had been estab-

blished—the deep-bodied, many-stringed viols with their silvery, subdued sound, and the shallow-bodied, four-stringed violins with their more penetrating timbre. Both persisted in the Baroque period, where they provided the nucleus of the orchestra; the treble violin, moreover, became the prima donna of the orchestra.

The violin, however, is not a child of the Baroque, but springs from earlier roots. Many of the great standard works on the history of the violin have only guesses to offer as to its origin, or they repeat legends not based on any evidence. In fact, the violin was not an "invention." Rather, it was the final product of a long and variegated process of development, a combination or fusion of many patterns and elements contributed by a number of different bowed instruments. Only when the great Lombard instrument makers in Brescia and Cremona took over, after the middle of the sixteenth century, did something like a standard form emerge (see Pl. 70)—standard, it is true, only in the sense of adherence to basic characteristics that still admitted countless variations of proportion, curvature, tonal quality, and so on. From that time on, we have something like a coherent history of the violin, found, if not in treatises, then at least in a considerable number of wonderful specimens that have survived to the present day. But the pre-history of the violin—that is, an account of its development before the time of the great violin makers in Brescia and Cremona—has not yet been written. Recently discovered facts[1] disclose that full-fledged violins—with shallow body, molded belly, upper, middle, and lower bouts, F holes, and spiral scrolls—must have existed as early as the second decade of the sixteenth century. We find abundant documentation in paintings of that time, i.e. in paintings by Gaudenzio Ferrari and his school in Lombardy and Piedmont. Thus it must have been about that time that the groping experimentation with shapes and sounds by imaginative instrument builders crystallized in the "final" form of the modern violin.

The lute is one of the most important and interesting instruments, and served throughout many centuries in various functions: for the accompaniment of singers, for the solo performance of music especially composed for it, and for the instrumental performance of part songs, in about the same way that polyphonic vocal or instrumental music is performed today on the piano.

The lute had a long and variegated history in the Orient before it was introduced to Europe through the spread of Islamic culture. The Arab origin is reflected in the names, derived from the Arab *Al'Ud* (the wood): *leüs, leuz, lus, lute, luth* (French), *laúd* (Spanish), *Laute* (German). In the Occident the drawings and miniatures in psalters, and especially the miniatures of Spanish manuscripts from the tenth to the thirteenth centuries, show an abundance of various shapes. The typical lute of the fifteenth century, which appears in countless Italian frescoes and altar paintings, was small with a short neck and a round, apple-shaped body. Around 1500, the lute grew and assumed the form which remained the classical one, of pear-shaped contour with a more shallow vaulted back composed of many ribs, and a broad neck which facilitated poly-

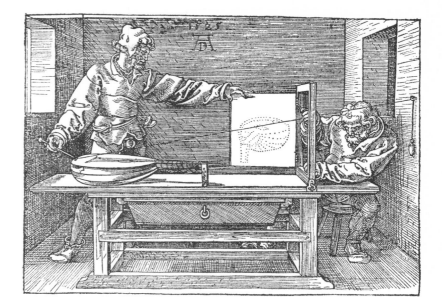

phonic playing (see Pl. 40). This form has been credited to the famous German lute maker Laux Maller, who worked in Belgium.

Symptomatic of the admiration in which the shape of the lute was held is the fact that it was one of the favorite objects for depiction in perspective, as many still lifes show, or its appearance in "The Ambassadors" by Holbein, or its use as a model for drawing in perspective as in a famous woodcut by Albrecht Dürer. (See Vignette above.) Dürer's father-in-law, Hans Frey of Nuremberg, was a famous lute maker and contemporary of Maller.

The sixteenth century abounds with names of famous lute makers, such as Pierre Lejeune, Jehan Helmur, Philippe Flac, Pierre Le Camus in France; and Wendelin Tieffenbrucker and Magnus Tieffenbrucker in Italy. Of seventeenth century lute makers, special mention is due Joachim Tielcke of Hamburg, who also excelled in building richly decorated guitars and viols (see Pl. 68).

However, as early as 1676, Thomas Mace in his amusingly loquacious *Musick's Monument* (London) laments the neglect of the lute. There, in a chapter called "The Lute Made Easy," the author addressed his beloved instrument:

> "What makes Thee sit so sad, my Noble Friend,
> As if Thou wert (with Sorrows) near Thy End?
> What is the Cause, my Dear Renowned Lute,
> Thou art of late so Silent, and so Mute?
> Thou seldom dost in Publick now appear;
> Thou art too Melancholy grown I fear."

The difficulty of tuning a lute was eloquently explained, or rather ridiculed, by Mattheson in his *Neu eröffnetes Orchester* (Hamburg, 1713). If a lute player lives to be eighty years old, said Mattheson, he certainly spends sixty years in tuning his instrument; and as for renewing strings and frets, and keeping the strings in order, he confessed to having heard reports from Paris that it cost the same amount there to keep a horse as a lute. But Mattheson seems to have had a slight aversion to the lute, in any case, and poked fun at the lute players of his time also, saying: "The flattering lutes have more partisans in the world than they merit, and the professors of lute playing are so unfortunate that if they scrape a few allemandes in the Viennese or Parisian fashion, they do not ask anything about the real musical art but boast with their own poverty."

The stringed keyboard instruments of the Renaissance, the harpsichord in its various forms and the clavichord, persisted into the sixteenth and the seventeenth centuries, gradually being adapted to the new needs. As solo instruments, they were still as useful as before for polyphonic pieces, but in addition they became indispensable to provide the *continuo*, the background harmony essential to the texture of Baroque music.

After the death of Handel and Johann Sebastian Bach, instruments changed in many directions. Some wind instruments such as the *oboe d'amore* and *oboe da caccia* became obsolete; the family of viols went out of fashion; and the delicate lute, after centuries of service in solo performance and as accompaniment for singers, yielded to sturdier rivals—first to the guitar,

and later to that indispensable piece of furniture in any bourgeois home from 1800 on, the pianoforte.

The "Sentimental Age" introduced a few new kinds of short-lived solo instruments. One was the baryton (see Pl. 83), a bass gamba that had, in addition to its six gut strings, numerous metal strings which vibrated sympathetically and could also be plucked by the left thumb. The sound of the baryton was highly praised by contemporaries for its fusion of the tone of gut and metal strings, and especially commended for the expression of gentle and melancholy emotions. Joseph Haydn wrote for his employer and protector, Prince Nikolaus Joseph Esterhazy, no less than 175 compositions (divertimenti, duos, sonatas, etc.) for this instrument. Another characteristic instrument of the Sentimental Age *(Empfindsamkeit)* was the glass harmonica, a set of glass bowls whose rims were set into vibration by the pressure of the fingertips. Its eerie and unearthly tone was highly appreciated at a time devoted to ethereal timbres and voices from the beyond. Also flutes—recorders as well as transverse flutes—and even violins were made in the form of walking sticks (Plate 80, 81) to enable the romantic wanderer to address the silver moon or compete with the nightingale, or if a more sober interpretation may be ventured here, to reinforce the persuasive charm of the travelling salesman.

Haydn, above all composers, taught the instruments "to speak"; the tendency was towards greatest possible expression, interesting tone color, and maximum volume. Mozart, in his later symphonies and chamber music, used the clarinet in an expressive way unparalleled heretofore; he also was the first to employ a certain type of alto clarinet, the basset horn (Plate 93), whose velvety sound is of a strange, sad beauty in some of his operas, the *Requiem*, and in his Freemason pieces.

But then during Beethoven's lifetime, a process of standardization and mechanization started that culminated in Wagner's and Richard Strauss's orchestras. Technologically, the decisive factors in this evolution were the oncoming industrialization and the sudden progress in metal manufacturing. The pianoforte, by means of metal reinforcement, became sturdier, larger, and louder; transverse flutes were made of metal and acquired an unparalleled playing flexibility with their new system of metal keys; the invention of rotary and piston valves for brass instruments stimulated a whole number of new types of instruments which were to be absorbed in military bands and in Wagner's giant orchestra.

Of course, many earlier instruments survived and were incorporated, in their original shape or in an "improved" one, into the modern orchestra. A remarkable case is that of the violin, which survives today with comparably minor changes in virtually the same shape given to it by the great Lombard masters. But even the violin has now become a product of standardized manufacture. And while, of course, any well-made precision tool possesses a kind of functional beauty, such as that of the saxophone or sarrusophone, the good old days of the individual craftsman who imparted to his creation his own particular handicraft secrets are over.

History of Collecting

In the great civilizations of Antiquity, such as China and Egypt, collections of musical instruments, in the broad sense of the word, must have been established with the formation of orchestras at courts and places of worship. It is reasonable to assume that the instruments, especially precious, highly decorated specimens, were kept in order and tune by the professional musicians employed at the court or temple. Israel, to mention only one example, had a body of professional musicians when David's temple was built; the Scriptures (Chronicles II, 5; 12–14) speak of 4,000 students of ritual music, with instruments of many kinds. According to Flavius Josephus the number was even larger at the time of the second temple. Some of the famous temple and court collections in the Far East, as for instance in China, Japan, and Indochina, have survived to our day.

In the Occident, during the Middle Ages, despite the existence of a great number of instruments, there is little evidence of large accumulations of instruments. This is not surprising considering the predominant style of instrumental music: performance by soloists and small ensembles. Exceptions must be assumed, however, if one takes into account certain pictorial evidence. The miniatures in the manuscripts containing the Cantigas de Santa Maria, collected at the court of Alfonso el Sabio of Castile (1252–1284), show so many beautifully adorned instruments, and so many different varieties within each basic type of instrument, that one may deduce that a substantial number of instruments were kept permanently at the court for the Christian, Moorish, and Jewish musicians employed there. If, on the other hand, a large number of instruments is also depicted, starting in the fourteenth century, in Italian and Flemish angel concerts, paintings as well as miniatures, this does not permit conclusions as to the existence of large orchestras or bodies of instruments; while the single instruments are, as a rule, represented with meticulous accuracy, their grouping into ensembles is largely the product of the painter's imagination.

In the Renaissance a differentiation between two types of collections begins to take place: a) a body of instruments kept together at church, convent, or palace for performance (Instrumentenkammer); and b) an aggregation of instruments collected as rare and curious objects, or for their exquisite workmanship and beauty, "pleasing the eye as well as the ear," which were kept as part or as a separate musical section of the Kunst- und Wunderkammer, or in special studi di musica. However, a sharp division between these two types, (a) and (b), cannot be drawn since often the showpieces also served performance purposes. Collections in the modern sense, systematically assembled and confined to instruments alone, cannot be dated prior to the Baroque.

Judging from contemporary sources about musical life and from the wealth of written instrumental music, the larger Renaissance courts must have had substantial collections containing both instruments used for performance and showpieces and curiosities.

While the Medici inventories of 1456 and 1492 contain a small number of instruments in comparison with the splendor reflected in later inventories of the Medici court, the court of

Mantua, thanks largely to the musical interests of Isabella d'Este and her passion for collecting, had a number of show-pieces, some of them commissoned from famous makers, others purchased from other courts. As for the musical riches in the castles of Urbino and Gubbio, the two residences of Federigo da Montefeltro, we can draw conclusions from the great number and variety of beautiful instruments represented in life size in the *trompe l'oeil* intarsias of the *studioli*. Precise historic evidence, in the form of inventories, of large and specialized collections can be traced back as far as the sixteenth century.

In France, Eugene de Bricqueville in his *Les Collections d'Instruments de Musique au 16, 17, 18 Siècles* mentions a fifteenth century Parisian collector, Maître Jacques Duchié whose *hôtel* in the Rue des Prouvelles contained harps, organs, vielles, guiternes, and psalterions.

In England, by far the largest collection was that belonging to Henry VIII. Besides several groups of English instrumentalists (minstrels and trumpeters), he employed various Spanish, Italian, and Dutch ensembles; and the inventory of his collections at his death included, as well as many bowed and plucked instruments, thirteen regals, seventeen virginals, and seventy-six recorders.

Italy, even earlier than 1600, abounded in collections of instruments. In Florence, the collection of instruments (*"liuti d'avorio e d'ebano, arpicordi, viole, cetere, flauti ed altri . . ."*) which formed part of the remarkable art collection of the sculptor Ridolfo Sirigatti, described in Raffaello Borghini's *Riposo* (1584), contained, side by side, ancient statues, Flemish landscapes, works by Sansovino and Michelangelo, and monstrous dried fish (*"mostri di pesci secchi naturali"*), conch shells, and the like. Venice was particularly rich in musical-instrument collections. Francesco Sansovino in his *Venezia Descritta* (1581) mentions no less than four *studi di musica*: the *studi* (music chambers) of the Cavaliere Sanudo; of Catarino Zeno, whose collection included a precious organ previously owned by King Mathias Corvinus of Hungary; of Luigi Balbi; and that of Agostino Amadi, containing *"non pure stromenti alla moderna ma alla Greca et all' antica,"* that is, archeological reconstructions which had become so fashionable with the rise of musical humanism in the late Quattrocento. One century later we know of the rich collection of the Procurator Contarini, of which parts are contained today in the Paris Conservatoire.

North of the Alps, the richest collections were in Augsburg, Graz, and near Innsbruck in the Tyrol. The one in Augsburg formed part of the rich art collection of the Fugger family. The inventory of Raimund Fugger, 1566, includes no less than 140 lutes, enumerating most of them in sets of three, four, or five, and frequently indicating the precious materials, such as ivory, ebony, brazilwood, fishbone, *canna d'India*, *ligno Queiaco*, of which they were made. Lutes, because of their delicate construction, elaborately carved sound holes, and use of precious materials in the staves forming their bellies, were among the great showpieces of the craft of the time.

A large *Instrumentenkammer* in Graz was established by the Archduke Karl of Styria; from its inventory (1577) one can conclude that it served chiefly performance purposes. Rich in rareties and precious showpieces, however, was the collection formed by the art connoisseur Archduke Ferdinand of Tyrol in his castle of Ambras near Innsbruck which he built to house his famous *Kunstkammer*, of which the musical instruments formed a special section (inventory 1596). The collection includes, among other rare and beautiful pieces, a bass cittern of fantastic, Gothic shape (Plate 6) from the fourteenth or fifteenth century; the beautiful cittern commissioned by the Archduke from Girolamo de Virchis of Brescia in 1574 (mentioned in the inventory as *"ain zitter an kragen die Lucretia Romana geschnitten"*); a bass lyra of the sixteenth century, actually a hybrid instrument combining the shape of an ancient lyre with a chitarrone neck, probably for use on the stage; several theorbos made by members of the Tieffenbrucker dynasty; numerous Renaissance lutes of German and Italian provenience; the unique set of five German Tartölten of the sixteenth century, bizarre wind instruments in dragon shape, probably used for masquerades; the inlaid chessboard containing a combination of regal and spinet, made by Anton Meidling, Augsburg, in 1587; an automatic spinet operated by a pin barrel, also made in Augsburg during the second half of the sixteenth century; two silver trumpets for fanfares made in Nuremberg in 1581 and 1657; a South German automat with moving figures of trumpeters and a little automatic regal concealed in the box; a Tyrolean organ-spinettina, second half of the sixteenth century, combining organ pipes of different tone with a spinettina (see Pl. 22); a sixteenth cen-

tury tournebout, probably Milanese; a unique set of four sixteenth century bass *sordoni*, probably Italian; and a collection of thirty miniature models of various instruments made during the sixteenth century.

In Milan the richest and most interesting collection of musical instruments was the musical section of the private museum of Manfredo Settala, described by Terzaghi (Museum Septalianum, Tortona, 1664), whose inventory enumerates fifty-nine instruments, among which were Oriental instruments brought back from Settala's travels, and unusual instruments constructed by himself. In Bologna, the museum founded by Ferdinando Cospi and described by Legati (Museo Cospiano, 1677) included a number of old and rare instruments.

Probably the most important Lombard collection dating back to the seventeenth century was that in the castle of Catajo near Padua which was built by Marchese Pio degli Obizzi. There, a museum, including a collection of musical instruments, was founded by his brother, Pio Enea, a friend of the famous Venetian art collector Teodoro Correr. After Pio Enea's death, the collection went to the ducal family of Modena, who enriched it substantially, and later to the Habsburg collections in Vienna where it was united, after World War I, with the Ambras collection under the supervision of Julius von Schlosser (who wrote the famous catalogue of the combined collections in 1920) in the Kunsthistorisches Museum. Among the rare and unique pieces in this collection are the German and Italian Renaissance lutes by such makers as Laux Maller, Hans Frey, and Wendelin Tieffenbrucker (Plate 13); early citterns

Castle Ambras near Innsbruck built by Archduke Ferdinand of Tirol (after a 19th century engraving.)

and the bizarre harp-cittern (Plate 14) by Wendelin Tieffen-brucker; the famous *lira da braccio* made by Giovanni d'Andrea of Verona in 1511; a consort of three *viole da gamba* made in 1580 by Gasparo da Salò; early Venetian violins; and numerous early North Italian woodwind instruments and cornetti. In Rome, at the same time, there existed the curious "Galleria Armonica" founded by the violone and trumpet player Michele Todini, and described in his *Dichiaratione* of 1676. Typical of the Baroque penchant for automats, it contained chiefly musical machines such as musical clocks, mechanical fiddles, and novel kinds of keyboard instruments, some of which were designed and built by himself. Another collection in Baroque Rome was in the Museo Kircheriano, which was founded by the great Jesuit scholar Athanasius Kircher. The collection formed the basis for the chapter on instruments in Kircher's *Musurgia Universalis* (1650), and for the treatise written by his pupil Filippo Bonnani, "*Gabinetto armonico pieno d'istromenti sonori indicati*" (1722).

The Medici collections mentioned earlier had expanded considerably since the fifteenth century; a yardstick of this growth is furnished by the inventory of 1716, signed by Bartolommeo Cristofori when he was appointed keeper of instruments at the Florentine court. Besides precious stringed and wind instruments, it included no less than fifty-three keyboard instruments (sixteen "cimbali;" twenty-one "spinette," "spinettoni," "spinettine;" and five organs). One single entry may be quoted here to show that more attention was given to the description of ornamentation than was required merely for identification: "A harpsichord from Antwerp with three principal stops, and one octave stop, and with two keyboards of ivory and ebony; with a case painted red, with gilded moldings; with the crossbar and the frontboard inlaid with rosettes of ivory and ebony and other designs, and the arms of the Ducal house of gilded wood in relief; and with an outer case painted red inside, with golden arabesques, and outside in pale blue, also with arabesques, with similarly decorated legs and a leather cover. No. 75."

The modern collections of musical instruments are too numerous to have their histories described here. The various reasons for their formation are extremely interesting, and we may single out as examples three of the largest and richest collections in order to throw some light on their origins: the collections in Vienna, Brussels, and New York.

The collection of instruments in the Vienna Kunsthistorisches Museum is at once the oldest and the youngest of the large collections. Its nucleus consists of two very old collections: one formed in the sixteenth century by Archduke Ferdinand of Tyrol and originally kept in the castle of Ambras in Tyrol; the other, the collection of the Lombard family of Obizzi, begun in the seventeenth century. But the merger of these two ancient components occurred only after the end of World War I. At that time Julius von Schlosser, an outstanding historian of Italian Renaissance art and also an enthusiastic chamber-music player and connoisseur of musical instruments and their history, had the ingenious idea of combining the Ambras and Obizzi collections of instruments into one public collection within the venerable Kunsthistorisches Museum. He wrote a catalogue (1920) which is still, after half a century, a standard work of solid and perceptive information about the evolution of instruments and their relation to successive styles of instrumental music.

The Musée Instrumental of the Conservatoire in Brussels is, in effect, the outcome of the work of Charles Mahillon, one of the great pioneers in the construction and manufacturing of new wind instruments in the nineteenth century. In 1846 the idea of this type of museum was proposed to the Royal Academy of Belgium. Soon thereafter the important collection of the renowned Belgian historian of music François Joseph Fétis was acquired by the state. In 1877, Victor Mahillon, the son and partner of Charles, became the first *conservateur*.

The largest American collection was formed neither by princes nor by professional manufacturers of instruments but by an amateur of vision and energy, Mrs. John Crosby Brown. It is the Crosby Brown Collection of Musical Instruments of all Nations, which has become part of the Metropolitan Museum of Art in New York. Mrs. Crosby Brown, a banker's wife, fell in love with some old Italian instruments and in 1884 began to collect instruments, at first somewhat indiscriminately but soon in a systematic fashion with the help of scholars and connoisseurs of all continents. Within two decades she had amassed a formidable and systematic collection of about 3,000 instruments. Today it numbers nearly 4,000, thanks to recent donations and purchases. The collections were given to the Metropolitan Museum of Art in installments, from 1889 to 1902, and the six-volume catalogue was completed in 1914. While this monument of American collecting cannot boast that it was derived from the *Kunst- und Wunderkammern* of the Renaissance, it has the rare merit of being conceived and organized along methodical principles, aiming at a complete and systematic representation of all families and types of instruments.

Organological Literature

The flow of organological literature proceeds in curious waves. The first comprehensive and systematic treatises on musical instruments were not written before the seventeenth century. The earliest one was Michael Praetorius's *Organographia*, published in Germany in 1618 at the beginning of the Thirty Years' War, which embodied the whole instrumentarium of the late Renaissance. It is still a gold mine of precise, well-organized information, and its picture section, the *"Theatrum Instrumentorum seu Sciagraphia,"* consists of woodcuts drawn with admirable accuracy on an exact scale and evidently executed under Praetorius's rigorous supervision. A *tabella universalis* gives the ranges of all string and wind instruments and, while it is restricted mainly to contemporary German ones, several exotic instruments are included such as Arab fiddles and even American trumpets and dance rattles, reflecting the expanding interest in the exotic world that had recently been opened by the conquistadores. It is at this same time that the *Kunst- und Wunderkammern*, the curio cabinets of princely collectors, began to include instruments from far lands.

In 1636–1637 the great Jesuit mathematician and theologian Father Marin Mersenne published his *Harmonie Universelle*, which contains, independently of Praetorius, many chapters on musical instruments illustrated by woodcuts and engravings of unequal accuracy. We find therein a new approach to scientific acoustics based on the radical progress of mathematics and physics at Mersenne's time. Mersenne based the explanations of the instruments on contemporary French practice, and references to English, German, and Italian methods of playing are rare.

While Mersenne was French to the bone in the organization of his thoughts, precise diction, and restriction to the French tradition in music, the next great treatise which appeared only thirteen years later incorporated new categories of musical information, showing an acquaintance with Oriental cultures transmitted to Rome by Catholic missionaries. This was the *Musurgia Universalis* by Athanasius Kircher, written in 1634. A polyhistor like Mersenne, Kircher brought to his study of musical instruments a deep interest in the history of the ancient world, especially its musical culture, and a remarkable knowledge in linguistics. Kircher also formed a large collection of instruments as part of the Museo Kircheriano at the Collegio Romano, which then became the material basis for a large picture book on instruments, the *Gabinetto armonico* (Rome, 1722), compiled by his pupil, Father Filippo Bonanni.

The eighteenth century produced a rich crop of books on musical instruments. There were monographs on single instruments, such as J. E. Altenburg's *Versuch einer Anleitung zur heroisch-musikalischen Trompeter- und Pauker-Kunst* (Halle, 1759); and (continuing in the tradition of Thomas Mace's seventeenth-century classical treatise on the lute, *Musick's Monument*) the many elaborate instruction books for playing, such as C. P. E. Bach's *Versuch über die wahre Art das Klavier zu spielen* (1753–1762), Leopold Mozart's *Versuch einer gründlichen Violinschule* (1756), and the numerous French *méthodes raisonées* for playing such instruments as the hurdy-gurdy and the musette. There were also treatises on the mechanics of the organ, and the first dictionaries of music in the modern sense appeared. But curiously enough, there were no general treatises on musical instruments of a comprehensive or encyclopedic nature comparable to the treatises of the seventeenth century. Even the famous supplement on musical instruments to Diderot and d'Alembert's *Encyclopédie*, published in Amsterdam in 1776–1777, with its many admirable engravings, was a guide to the making of instruments rather than an encyclopedic survey.

Nor did the nineteenth century, that golden age of historical schools and historians, such as Macaulay, Lord Acton, Michelet, Taine, Ranke, Mommsen, and pioneer historians of music such as Ambros, leave us a comprehensive history or dictionary of musical instruments, even though it was the century when the great collections were formed in such places as Brussels, Vienna, Stockholm, and New York.

But the end of the nineteenth century and the first years of the twentieth witnessed a sudden flood of historical monographs on all important instruments—an unprecedented outburst in organological literature, and an impressive indication of the deepening of historical interest in instruments, which continues unabated to our day and has resulted in numerous comprehensive dictionaries and histories of musical instruments.

Classification

A clear-cut and consistent classification of musical instruments which would take into account instruments both of the past and present, not only in Europe, but in the rest of the world as well, is not an easy task. Many classifications have been tried with varying success. A list based on the shape of the instrument would be confusing, since the number and variety of forms is virtually limitless, and since there exists, besides a large number of familiar, standardized forms, an immense profusion of bastard and transitional forms. Similarly problematic would be a system based on the materials of which the instruments are built (as for instance "brass instruments"), since the variety of minerals and metals, woods and other plant fibers, bones, hides, and shells is limitless, and since, furthermore, many instruments employ more than one substance. A classification according to the playing method, (such as "percussion instruments") is bound to be inconsistent, since many instruments are played in more than one manner, and since many instruments have changed their method of playing throughout history (for instance, members of the lute family have been bowed as well as plucked). Today the most widely accepted classification is the one suggested by Erich v. Hornbostel and Curt Sachs which is based on the various devices that actually generate the sound. These devices are:

1. Vibrating strings (stringed instruments or chordophones).
2. Vibrating air columns (wind instruments or aerophones).
3. Vibrating membranes, as in drums with skin heads (membranophones).

4. Matter vibrating without the aid of strings, air, or membranes (idiophones or autophones) such as slit drums, bells, gongs, chimes, xylophones, the African zanze, musical glasses, rattles, scrapers, etc.

Chordophones are usually subdivided into plucked, struck, and bowed strings or, more practically, into four general groups:

a) Zithers have neither neck nor yoke; the strings are stretched between the two ends of a body which may be a shallow box, a tube, or a stick equipped with additional resonators such as gourds.

b) Lutes, in the general sense of the term, have a sound box terminating in a neck which serves both as a handle and as a device for extending the strings beyond the sound box. (Into this category fall plucked lutes and bowed lutes such as violins, viols, etc.)

c) Harps are instruments whose strings, invariably plucked, do not run parallel to the soundboard, but vertically away from it.

d) Lyres have strings which run parallel to the soundboard but continue beyond it to a crossbar or yoke held by two arms projecting from the sound box. The ancient Greek lyra was a bowl lyre with a soundboard of skin stretched over a shallow bowl made of wood or the back of a turtle shell. The ancient Greek kithara used a box made of wooden front, back, and side walls joined together.

But however closely woven is the net of classification, there are many transitional and hybrid forms of stringed instruments

"Atelier de Luthier" (*from a French engraving, eighteenth century.*)

which are not caught in its meshes. Such forms include the English harp-lute and harp-guitar, invented by Edward Light in London around 1800, and the French lyre-guitars of the eighteenth century and Empire – fashionable ladies' instruments that combined the soundboard, arms, and yoke of a lyre with a central finger board for stopping the strings in guitar fashion.

The wind instruments are usually divided into woodwind and "brass" instruments, a practical classification that suffices for the modern orchestra but does not do justice to the functional characteristics and the great variety of materials that have been used for making such instruments in various periods. Flutes and certain reed pipes are made also of bone, clay, stone, metal, glass, and bamboo, while trumpets and horns are frequently made from materials such as clay, wood, and even tree bark. A more scientific classification, as suggested by Nicholas Bessaraboff, divides the wind instruments into three categories according to the fundamental method of tone production:

a) Flue-blown – instruments in which the air stream is shaped and directed by a "flue," either the lips of the player, as in vertical and transverse flutes, or a canal mouthpiece, as in recorders;

b) Reed-vibrated – those pipes equipped with a double reed, such as the ancient aulos, the Renaissance shawm, the modern oboe and bassoon, or with a single reed, such as the clarinet and the saxophone;

c) Lip-vibrated – those in which the player's lips themselves function as vibrator, in combination with a special mouthpiece,

such as trumpets and horns – in short, all instruments that are commonly called "brass."

A further subdivision within these three main groups according to acoustical properties, such as range, shape of tube, and the various devices for lengthening and shortening the tube, is beyond the range of this book. An excellent classification can be found in Nicholas Bessaraboff's *Ancient European Musical Instruments* (Harvard University Press, 1941).

Membranophones can be classified in various ways, for instance according to the quality and range of tones they produce, or the method by which the player puts them into action. Many drums, such as the tabor and the side drum, produce only rhythmic sound (i. e., one tone rhythmically repeated); others, such as the kettledrum, produce a scale or at least a number of tones of different pitch. And as for action, there are drums operated by players' hands, or beating rods, or by keyboards, as in the drum stops of large organs, or by automats, or by the wheels of the carriage which transports them, as in an invention by Leonardo da Vinci.

An enormous wealth of shapes, materials, sounds, and playing methods, finally, is represented by the large group of idiophones. Here we find bells, gongs, cymbals, castanets, the jew's harp, xylophones, and others. The most logical principle of classification for this group seems, again, that between instruments producing chiefly rhythmic, unpitched sounds, such as cymbals and castanets, and those which provide tones of definite pitch, as for instance bells and xylophones.

Riccho son d'oro,

et riccho son di suono,

Non mi sonar si tu non ha del buono.

(I'm rich in gold and I'm rich in sound,

O touch me not if no good tune is found.)

(Inscription on a Spinettino

made for Eleonora della Rovere,

Venice, 1540)

2 *Lur*

6th century B.C., found in Husby, Denmark

Most instruments preserved from prehistoric times or from antiquity are made of stone, clay, bone, or horn; few are of wood or metal. The exceptions are those instruments preserved under unusually favorable conditions – for instance, the wooden harps, lutes, and lyres found sealed up in the tombs of Egypt or the Near East, where the climate is very dry. Another favorable environment was the moors of southern Scandinavia, which have yielded, since 1797, a remarkable number of Bronze Age metal instruments – the *lurer*, of which no less than nineteen are now in the National Museum in Copenhagen.

The tube of the *lur* and its flat disc at the lower end, which apparently projected above the player's head, are cast with admirable craftsmanship. The tube gradually increases in diameter from the mouthcup to the disc, and it is reinforced by many bands or rings of bronze. The mouthcup, unlike that of modern metal instruments, is not detachable.

The *lur* has presented many problems to the historian. Assumptions about its age have differed, ranging from 3000 *B. C.* to the sixth century *B. C.* Its shape has been likened to that of mammoth tusks (which may have been its original material) since the curvature of the

tube makes a complex twist not restricted to one plane; *lurer* were often found in pairs, showing a symmetrical twist in opposite directions, like the two horns of an ox.

Also controversial is the question of their use: for cult purposes, or as a war instrument, or in both ways. Even the timbre and range of the *lur* have been much discussed; it produces a rough and shrill sound, but its surprisingly elaborate mouthpiece permits tones up to the eleventh harmonic, and a German publication of 1933 even went so far as to claim the *lurer* as evidence of Teutonic "polyphony 3000 years ago."

The helmet *(Vikso)* in our illustration has ox horns whose contortions parallel those of a pair of *lurer*.

Copenhagen, National Museum.

VII   *Tromba curua*

3 *English Medieval Gittern*

See page 49/50 This gittern is probably the earliest preserved, and certainly the most beautiful, Medieval stringed instrument. Its body, made of boxwood, is of highly complex shape and quite different from that of a Renaissance cittern or gittern, of which there are still many examples extant.

In side view, the instrument resembles a dolphin, with a deep head and a body tapering towards the tail end. The side walls, very small at the tail end, grow progressively towards the end with the finger board, so that the body gains size rapidly until it reaches a depth which is more than one-quarter its total length. At the larger end, just where the later citterns had their thin neck, the body narrows to a thin vertical wall perforated by a large oval hole and terminating in a winged dragon. The hole enabled the player's hand to grasp the neck in such a way that the fingers could stop the strings; the instrument could also thus be suspended or hung on the wall. In the later Italian Quattrocento citterns this feature was reduced to a hook at the back of the neck, which was retained in citterns for still another century. The perforated wall of our gittern, while greatly increasing the area available for the woodcarver, must have very much limited the motion of the stopping fingers. The side walls are so massive that they inevitably dull the tone, another reason why the instrument must have excelled as a showpiece rather than in performance.

The back of the gittern is keel-shaped, with two planes meeting at the axial ridge. Looking at the instrument from the top, we see an outline comprising no less than five curves. Accordingly, the side walls are divided into five vertical sections separated by carved strips, and the kind and subject of carved decoration changes from section to section. The carving is masterly indeed; it extends over all the side walls, the tail pin, and the lower side of what we call the perforated wall, well into the keel-shaped back. The style of the carvings can profitably be compared with English sculptures and manuscript illuminations of the early fourteenth century. Some of the figures, such as that of an archer with the hind legs of a lion, parallel the monsters teeming in the margins of fourteenth century Books of Hours. The body and neck of the instrument are made from a single piece of wood and carved in decorated panels of foliage inhabited by huntsmen, foresters, wild animals, and grotesques. Great care has been taken to represent different kinds of foliage in the various panels.

The addition of a violin soundboard, with F holes, bridge, finger board, and string holder, to this venerable instrument is something of a shock to the eye. It is not certain when this was done. However, a silver stud in the tail pin bears the inscription "1578," when, in all probability, some restorations may have been made. From a silver cover for the pegbox showing the arms of Queen Elizabeth I and her favorite, Robert Dudley, Earl of Leicester (who derived his pedigree from the Earls of Warwick), one can assume that the instrument was at some time owned by one of them. Only recently this gittern found its permanent home in the British Museum.

London, British Museum. Purchase made possible with the aid of contributions from the Pilgrim Trust, the National Collections Fund, and a special Treasury grant.

4 **Fiddle**

North Italian, 14th century

This famous, elaborately carved instrument of boxwood comes closest in form to the rebec of *See page 51* the late Middle Ages and the Renaissance. The rebec had a cucumber- or pear-shaped body and a sickle-shaped pegbox; it was played with a bow and was chiefly used to play dance music. The present specimen has a wide finger board, and the whole width of the soundboard is taken up by a Gothic rose of interlacing ribbons of wood. Furrows at the nut and five pin holes at the tail reveal that at one time the instrument was furnished with five strings; the pegs are missing.

The back of this instrument is completely carved in deep relief, from the pegbox, through neck and body, down to the tail end. The sickle-shaped head is carved in the form of a leaf and includes the figure of a sitting woman with a little lute in her hands. An animal head and a standing figure holding a scroll are shown on the neck, with Gothic leaves beneath. On the central section of the back we see a pair of young lovers, arm in arm; the well-dressed youth carries a falcon, and a little dog plays at the feet of the lady, while in the foliage above the lovers, a cupid arches his bow. At the lower end, a stag leaps. The eyes of the human figures as well as of the animals are set with little pieces of white bone. The carving is done in undercutting on very thick walls, a fact which no doubt impaired the tone of the instrument.

New York, Irwin Untermyer Collection.

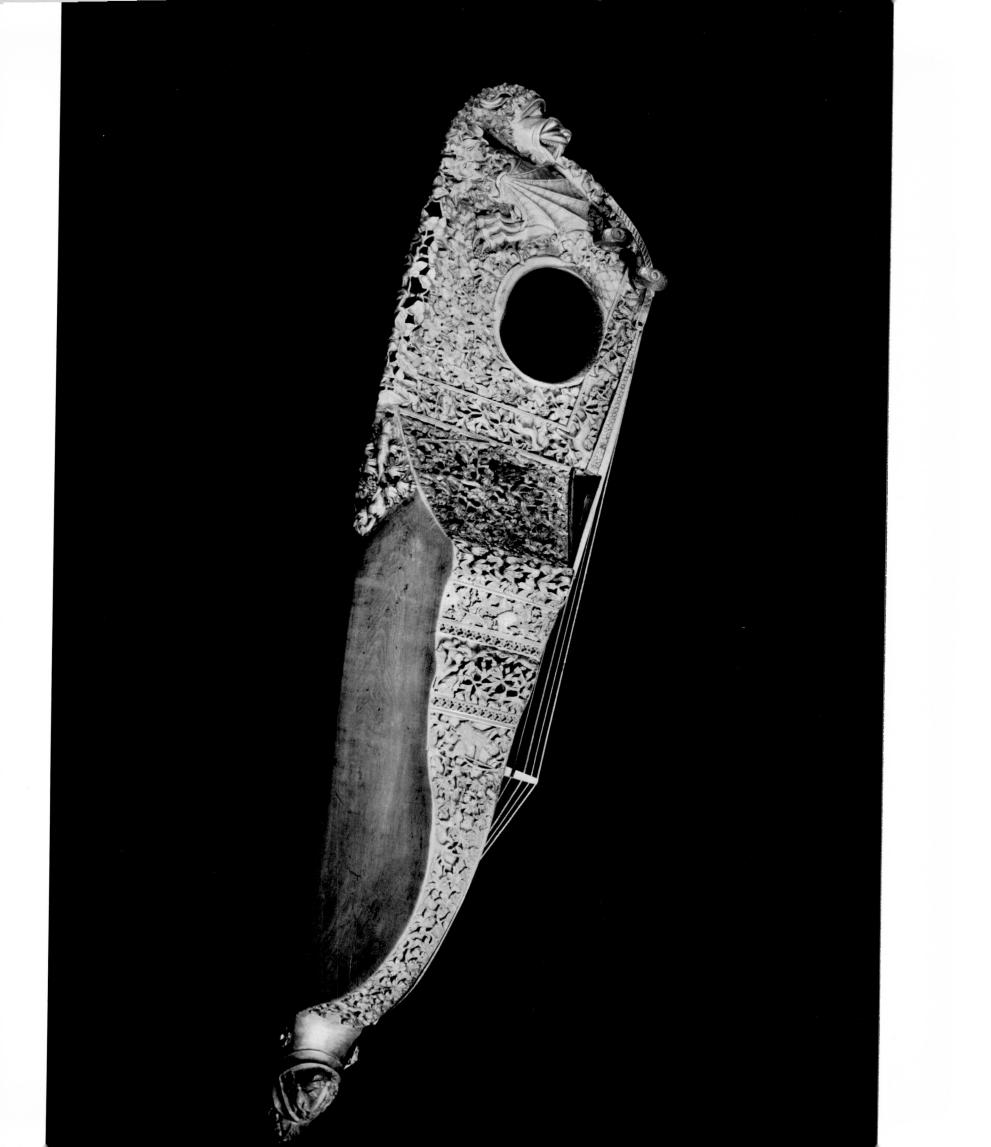

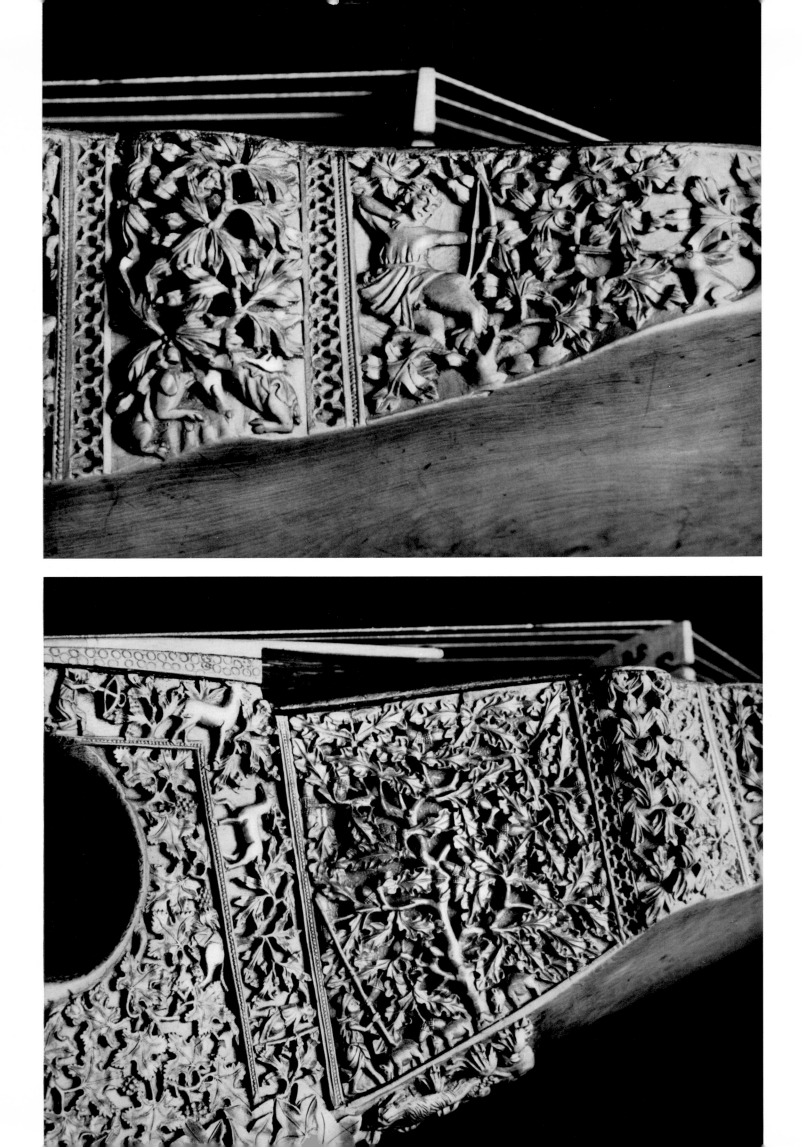

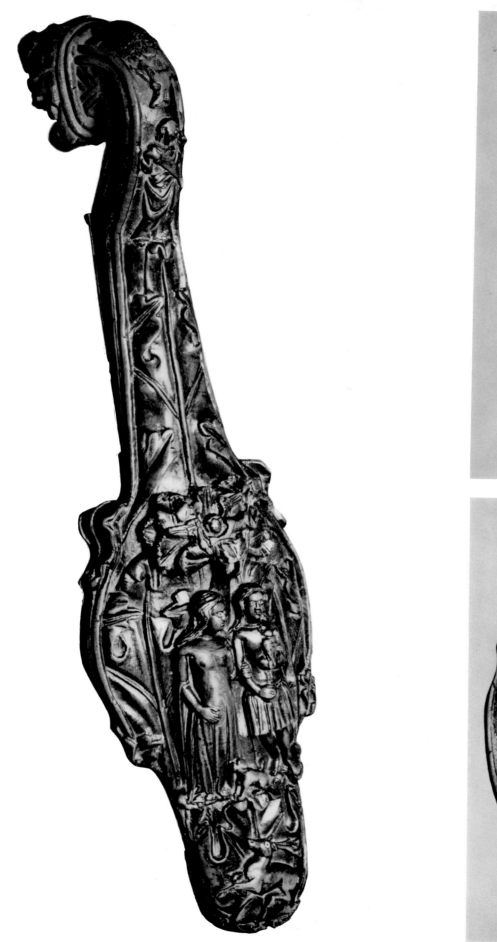
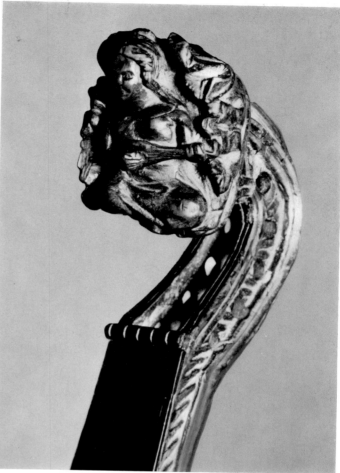

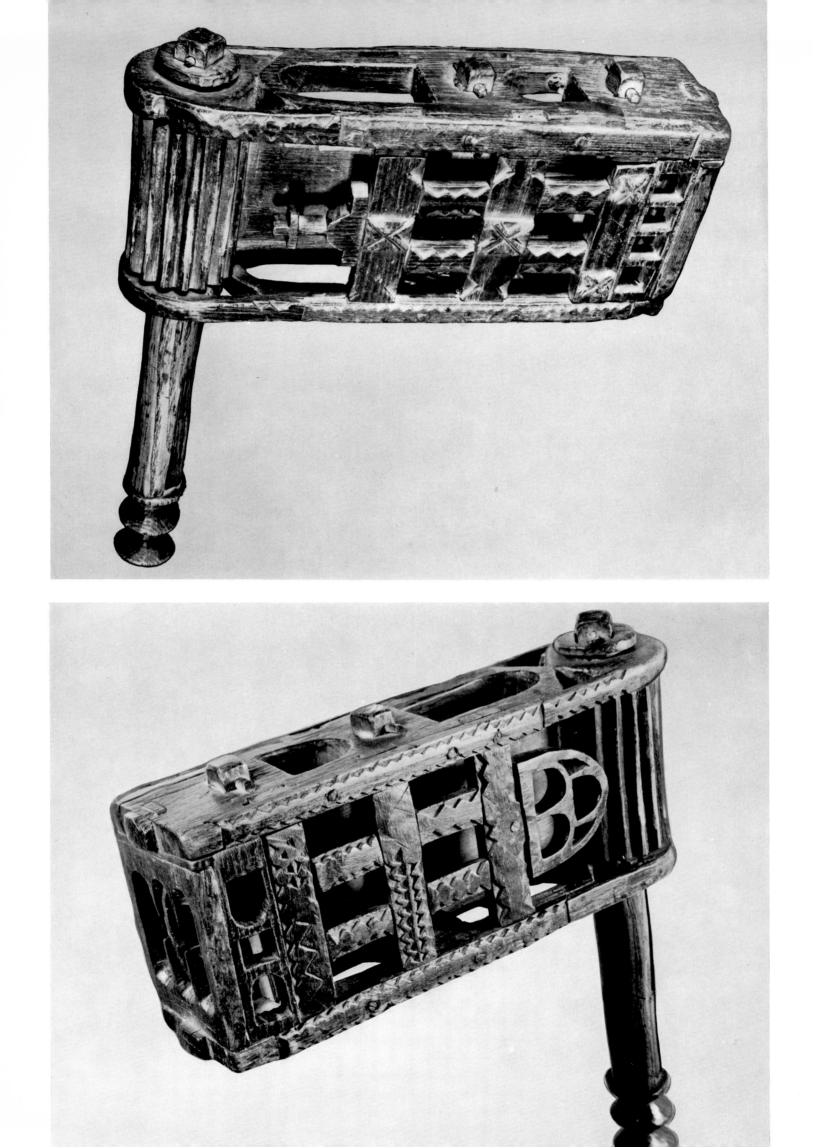

5 *Crecelle*

French, 15–16th century

According to Catholic usage, the church bells had to remain silent during Holy Week and, as an old legend has it, they "flew to Rome" for that time. Thus they had to be replaced, during the celebration of the Mass and at other times, by another instrument – the crecelle – a sort of wooden rattle.

The construction of the crecelle was fairly simple: the handle is connected with a fluted cylinder or cogwheel, and with a box which holds one or more wooden tongues whose edges touch the indentations of the cylinder. When the player, holding the handle, whirls the crecelle, the wooden tongues are caught by the cogwheel and in snapping back they create a loud, burring noise. Illustrations of crecelles, together with other forms of rattles, are found occasionally in late Medieval and Renaissance Books of Hours, often shown in the hands of musician-monsters among the drolleries which decorate the margins of the pages.[2]

Actually the crecelle is only one of many kinds of wheel-rattles used for many popular purposes, such as making carnival noises. Modern composers have availed themselves of the symbolic connotations of rattles, and incorporated them in their orchestra: thus we find their sound in Richard Strauss's *Till Eulenspiegel*, Maurice Ravel's *L'Enfant et les sortilèges*, and Ottorino Respighi's *Pini di Roma*.

The crecelle shown here is one of the earlist preserved, of beautiful workmanship and still embodying Gothic design in the construction of the cagelike box and the carving.

New York, Metropolitan Museum of Art, 54.160 (gift of Blumka Gallery, 1954).

6 *Basslute*

German (probably), ca. 1500

This unique and remarkably well-preserved instrument is actually, in both shape and construction, quite different from ordinary Renaissance lutes. Nor does it correspond to Renaissance citterns, which all show a characteristic tapering in the depth of the body from top to bottom. However, here we call this instrument a lute because of its two unmistakable lute necks with their characteristic sharp bend, and also because it has been called a lute as early as the Ambras inventory of 1596, in which it is mentioned as one of the treasures of the *Kunstkammer: "mer ain grosse selczame lauten mit zween krägen und drei stern."*

The instrument is of astonishing size, its length 175.5 cm and its depth 7 cm at the shoulders, gradually increasing to 19 cm at its lower end. The most striking feature is its asymmetry; its right side consists of a series of forceful curves, a pattern that reminded Julius Schlosser (in his catalogue of the Vienna collection) of "Gothic form-fantasy"; the lower end also forms a sweeping curve to the side. The soundboard, made of spruce, has three small sound holes with roses in a Gothic tracery design. Side walls and back are of maple, and treated with a reddish-brown varnish. There are three sets of strings: four double drones are attached to four small wooden bars in the lower part of the soundboard and reach up to the pegs in the shorter of the two necks; six pairs of stopped strings are attached to bars in the upper part of the soundboard and, at their opposite end, to the pegs in the longer neck; finally there are three single short treble strings. The latter are likewise attached to small bars on the soundboard and reach to three single pegs that are not part of the pegboxes but are inserted in the top of the right shoulder. The arrangement of separate bridges is quite unusual and recalls similar devices used in some early keyboard instruments. Even more striking is the manner of fretting: the frets consist of little, separate, teethlike blocks of wood near the place where each pair of strings should be stopped.

Sammlung alter Musikinstrumente, Kunsthistorisches Museum, Vienna (Schlosser Catalogue No. A. 60). Background: T8471 (or T8417?) – Baldachin, gold and silver brocade, french, early 18th century, Oesterreichisches Museum für Angewandte Kunst, Vienna.

7 *Altolute*

by Georg Gerle, Innsbruck, ca. 1580

The characteristic feature of this Renaissance lute is its beautiful back, composed of eleven ivory strips separated by black lines The narrow neck and pegboard are likewise made of ivory. An elegant Renaissance rose decorates the soundboard (not shown); and there are five double strings, one single treble string, and eight gut frets.

The printed maker's label inside the instrument says: "Georg Gerle, fürstlicher Durchlechtig/keit chalkandt zu Ynnsprugg." ("Calcant" was the name for the men who worked the bellows of church organs by stepping on them.) Gerle, of whose life little is known, was instrument maker for the court chapel of Duke Ferdinand of Tyrol in Innsbruck, and probably earlier in Prague. This lute is included in the Ambras inventory of 1596 and was probably used by the Duke himself; it was expertly restored at the beginning of the nineteenth century.
Sammlung alter Musikinstrumente, Kunsthistorisches Museum, Vienna (Schlosser Catalogue No A 35.)

8 *Cittern*

by Girolamo de Virchis, Brescia, 1574 · Made for Duke Ferdinand of Tyrol (d. 1596).

This instrument is one of the loveliest stringed instruments extant, a priceless example of Lombard artistry of the sixteenth century. Every minute detail of the carved and painted decor is made with exquisite workmanship, yet all these details blend together in a harmonious whole.

This cittern is the only known piece made by Girolamo de Virchis, of whom little is recorded except that he worked as *citeraro* in Brescia in the second half of the sixteenth century. Duke Ferdinand of Tyrol, who ordered the instrument, was a musical connoisseur and, in his castle of Ambras, near Innsbruck, owned a precious collection of musical manuscripts, as well as a *Musikkammer* containing many instruments for practical performance and a *Kunstkammer* containing his art objects, among which was a small but choice group of musical instruments of outstanding beauty. The inventory taken after the death of Duke Ferdinand in 1596 describes our piece as, "ain Zitter, an Kragen die Lucretia Romana geschnitten" (a cittern whose neck shows a carving of the Roman Lucretia).

The body of the instrument is made of Palisanderwood, with the back composed, in fan fashion, of eight strips of wood of alternating grain. A red-yellow varnish bestows great luminosity on the instrument. The soundboard is perforated by a large hole in which is set a carved, painted, and gilded ornament including putti, sphinxes, griffins, masks, and the Tyrolian eagle. On one side of the lower end of the finger board the little figure of a nude woman is growing out, as it were, from a snail shell. The traditional round protuberances at the shoulders of the instrument are of elaborate leaf design. At the point where the neck begins, the upper end of the back is hidden under the ornate coat of arms of Duke Ferdinand, which includes two nymphs upholding the ducal hat.

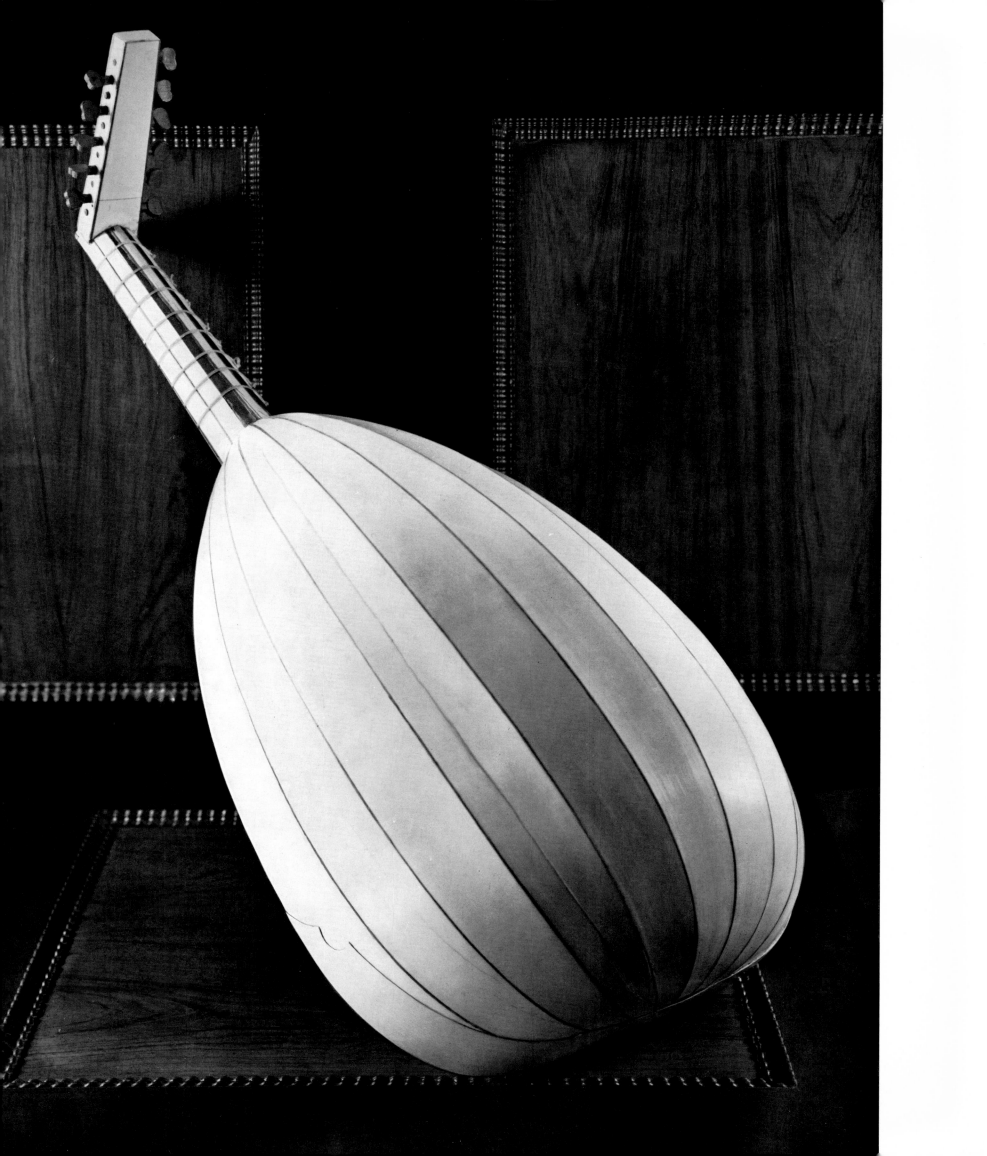

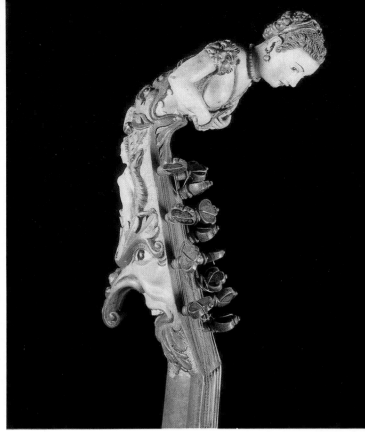
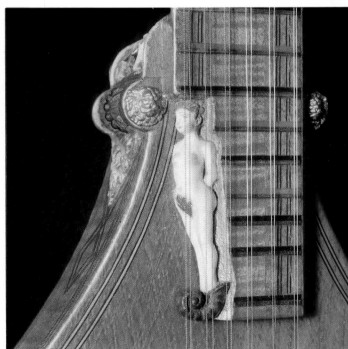

The pièce de resistance, however, is the head of the instrument: a dragon's head, from whose mouth emerges the nude and jewel-covered half-figure of Lucretia stabbing herself with a dagger. Two natural pearls decorate her ears. The back of the pegbox also shows a nude woman, comparable to the one decorating the fingerboard. Beneath her is a grimacing, open-mouthed monster head whose large, projecting nose forms the hook required in every cittern of that time.

Sammlung alter Musikinstrumente, Kunsthistorisches Museum, Vienna (Schlosser Catalogue No. A 61). Background: T 8509 – Pluviale, silver brocade, french, mid-18th century. Oesterreichisches Museum für Angewandte Kunst, Vienna.

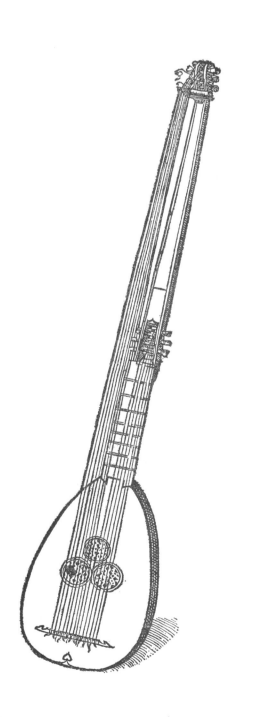

9 *Chitarrone*

Inscribed: "Franciscus de Raynaldis an 1508" (but probably dating from the end of the 16th century).

The chitarrone was one of several forms of bass lutes which developed out of the lute towards the end of the sixteenth century. Besides their melody strings, they all have a number of long bass strings running outside the fingerboard, necessitating a second pegbox. The chitarrone had the longest neck of all the bass lutes, often more than twice the length of the body. The fingerboard was broad, as in lutes, to facilitate the stopping of strings; but instead of bending back, it continued straight into the lower of the two pegboxes. From there, the neck continued in diminishing width toward the second pegbox, which accommodated the bass strings.

The instrument shown here has eleven melody and six bass strings. Its back is composed of twenty-three ribs of alternating ebony and ivory. The soundboard has a large sound hole of three-leaf-clover shape, set with a rose of geometric tracery. The fingerboard and the back of the neck are richly inlaid in ivory and ebony, with exquisite grotesque ornament; and the upper pegbox terminates in a carved head.

The chitarrone was used for the accompaniment of singers and as a bass instrument in the orchestra. Its picturesque form was favored by painters of the seventeenth and eighteenth centuries; and the long neck forms a striking diagonal plane in allegorical and genre paintings of Caravaggio, Rombouts, Honthorst, and Watteau, to mention only a few.

Copenhagen, Carl Claudius' Samling af Gamle Musikinstrumenter (No. 106).

10 *Lira da Braccio*

by Giovanni d'Andrea, Verona, 1511 · Inscribed: "Joannes Andree. Veronen...nosto (agosto?) 1511"

The lira da braccio was one of the most important and beloved instruments in Italy in the fifteenth and sixteenth centuries. It was used for the solo performance of polyphonic music, but even more for the accompaniment of recitatives. The singer usually improvised his own

61

accompaniment by adding one or more instrumental lines to that of his own voice. Leonardo da Vinci was one of the many celebrated performers on this instrument; when, as a young man, he moved from Florence to Milan to enter the service of the Duke Lodovico Sforza, he brought with him a lira da braccio which he himself had made, partially of silver, in the shape of a horse's skull.[3]

With its flat body, rounded shoulders, and unique arrangement of strings, the lira da braccio differed from the contemporary viola da gamba, which had a deep body and sloping shoulders. In addition to five melody strings which could be stopped against the finger board, the lira da braccio had two "drone" or bourdon strings that ran freely through the air outside the finger board (held there by a little wooden stick protruding from the pegbox), which could sound only their full length, or one tone, when touched by the bow or plucked by the player's fingers. It was probably these free strings which accounted for the name lira (lyre).

The most characteristic part of the lira da braccio was its head, sometimes a heart- or leaf-shaped wooden board and sometimes – in more richly decorated specimens – a whole box with a cover at its rear. But whatever the shape of the head, the method of attaching the strings was the same: the seven pegs were inserted from the front, rather than from the side as in viols or the later violins; and the strings were fastened to the small ends of the pegs which protruded from the rear of the head. In order to be thus fastened, the five melody strings were made to pass from the nut through little holes to the back of the pegboard.

Renaissance treatises tell us of the importance of the lira da braccio as an instrument of the virtuosi and humanists, for performance not only of contemporary but also of ancient poetry. No wonder that specimens were made with highly original and unique decoration – instruments that were admired as the very summit of craftsmanship. One of these has survived the only extant piece by its maker and the earliest of the few remaining lire da braccio.

The body of this instrument has a tripartite outline like the violin with upper, middle, and lower bouts, but the curvature of the contour is quite unlike that of the later instrument. The tail end is markedly curved up in the center and thus divided into two semicircular curves. The middle bouts are comparatively shallow and their corners are not sharply pointed. The shoulders are sloping but curve upward in the middle, forming little spirals that recall the scrolls at the shoulders of Renaissance citterns (see Plate 8). Hollowed out by the carving knife, the side walls are slightly convex.

The soundboard of our lira da braccio is of a warm brown color, while the back and sides have a dark reddish varnish. The finger board and the string holder are decorated in typical North Italian style, alla certosina – that is, by a colorful combination of ebony, ivory, bone which has been stained green, and brown wood. The most striking feature, however, is the carving of belly and back, which give the impression of human forms. The belly is shaped like a male torso and, correspondingly, the front of the pegbox shows a grotesque male face. The back shows, in stronger relief, the form of a female torso, with breasts and nipples strongly marked; and, accordingly, the back of the pegbox shows a woman's face. But this is not the end of the sculptural fantasy: acanthus leaves encroach upon the female torso, and on its middle region is a large moustachioed mascherone that overlaps the undulations of the female form. The sound holes in the belly are unusually large, of tendril shape; the pegbox can be closed, and it is remarkable how cleverly the pegs are inserted so as to disturb as little as possible the grimace of the grotesque face. A little ivory plaque inserted into the back bears the somewhat miswritten Greek inscription: "ΛΥΠΗΣ ΙΑΤΡΟΣ ΕΣΤΙΝ ΑΝΘΡΩΠΟΙΣ ΩΑΗ".

It actually quotes an ancient monostichon: "Men have song as the physician of pain," thus paying respect to humanist learning, so important in Venetian culture of the time.

How far this masterpiece of applied sculpture is from the standardized forms of string instruments of later ages! And how much it helps us to visualize other Renaissance instruments,

such as the lira da braccio that Leonardo built in the shape of a horse's skull—a shape so beloved by that great connoisseur of animal anatomy!

Sammlung alter Musikinstrumente, Kunsthistorisches Museum, Vienna (Catalogue by Julius Schlosser, No. C. 94).

11 *Lira da Gamba*

Inscribed : "Antonius Brensius Bonon 1592" ("Bonon" meaning "Bononiensis" or "of Bologna")

The form of the *lira da gamba* recalls somewhat that of a violoncello, with its marked middle bouts and sharply projecting corners; but it has a broader shape and four sharp ridges running diagonally from the soundboard to the corners. The sound holes are not of F shape but are a complex version of C holes. There is also a round sound hole high on the soundboard near the end of the finger board, with a rose which has been reconstructed. Bridge, string holder, neck, finger board, and pegbox are modern but excellent reconstructions. Unfortunately, no other instruments by this maker are known.

The *lira da gamba* was the tenor-sized version of the *lira da braccio* (see Pl. 10 and 12). It was considerably larger and equipped with several more strings, sometimes as many as sixteen. This instrument has eleven melody strings and two drones, or bourdons. The large *lire* developed after 1500 and were in fashion for about a century, almost exclusively in Italy.

Leipzig, Karl-Marx-Universität (Kinsky Catalogue No. 782).

12 *Lira da Braccio*

by Giovanni Maria da Brescia, 1540

This elegant instrument can profitably be compared with the much more ornate *lira da braccio* by Giovanni d'Andrea (Pl. 10). Most characteristic of the *lira da braccio* shape is the large, richly decorated pegbox with its seven frontal pegs for the five melody strings and two drones, and also the incurved contour of the tail end.

The *lira da braccio* was made in many different shapes. This one approaches that of the violin in several ways, principally due to its flat body with the side walls divided, much more sharply than the d'Andrea instrument, into upper, middle, and lower bouts, and also to the existence here of F holes. (An instrument similar to this one is played by Apollo in Lionbruno's "Contest of Apollo and Marsyas," a painting once in the Kaiser-Friedrich-Museum, Berlin, but unfortunately destroyed in World War II.) It has been said that the violin developed directly out of the *lira da braccio*[4]; but the available evidence reveals that these two bowed instruments existed for some time side by side, serving different musical purposes.[3]

By courtesy of the Ashmolean Museum, Oxford.

64

13 *Basslute*

*by Wendelin Tieffenbrucker, Padua, 1595 · Inscribed, "Padova 1595 Wendelio Venere";
marked "WT," with the sign of the anchor*

At the threshold of the Baroque era, new musical forms and textures stimulated radical changes in many traditional instruments. Among them was the lute family, which developed bass members to satisfy the demand for continuo instruments in the orchestra, especially that of the newborn opera. The main result of the development of bass lutes such as the therbo and the chitarrone was the addition of a second pegbox to hold the long bass strings which ran outside the finger board. But other ways were also tried: the builder of this instrument arrived at a unique solution by elongating the body rather than the neck; and the three single bass strings pass over the finger board as well as the long soundboard, to a small string holder glued to the soundboard. The seven pairs of melody strings are attached to another string holder.

The soundboard has two beautiful roses: a small round one of foliate scroll design, and a large oval one with an emblem including a rampant lion. The back of the instrument (not shown) is composed of twenty-five ribs. The size of this bass lute is remarkable; it has a total length of 147 cm—about the average length of a chitarrone (see Pl. 9). However, in the chitarrone the body comprises about one-third the total length of the instrument, while in our bass lute, the body takes up more than two-thirds of the whole.

Of Wendelin Tieffenbrucker little is known except that many beautiful instruments made by him are preserved, with labels dating from 1572 to 1611.

Sammlung alter Musikinstrumente, Kunsthistorisches Museum, Vienna (Schlosser Catalogue No. A.46)

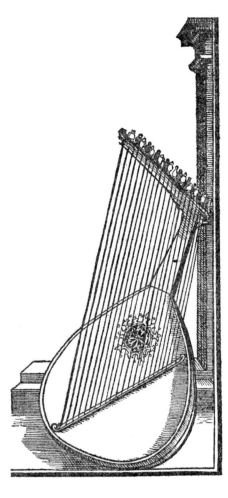

14 *Harp-Cittern*

by Wendelin Tieffenbrucker, Padua, second half of the 16th century.
Inscribed, "In Padova Wendelio Venere de Leonardo Tieffenbrucker"

This unusual instrument is the only one of its kind surviving, and perhaps even the only one made. Basically – that is, in the shape of its body, its fretted neck, and the form of its pegbox – it is a cittern. But it has many more strings than a cittern – enough, in fact, to occupy almost the whole width of the soundboard. This is made possible by two attachments. One is a curved, harp-shaped arm swinging away from the nut of the instrument and carrying twenty long open strings. The other attachment is a row of tuning pins on the right shoulder carrying fifteen short strings. The middle section of strings, attached to the pegs of the pegbox, forms the ordinary cittern equipment: two single bass strings, six double strings, and one chantarelle. The total number of strings is no less than forty two. This combination and grouping of the strings represents a solution to the problem solved already in a simpler way by the instrument on Plate 6.

There were many hybrid instruments which, like this one, combined features of different main types, and which defy the attempts of historians to make simple classifications of instruments into a few clearly distinct families. Examples somewhat comparable to our harp-cittern include the harp-lute shown by Praetorius in his Theatrum Instrumentorum (1618) in Tafel 36, and a whole cluster of "combination" instruments invented in the first part of the nineteenth century in England by Edward Light and others: harp-lutes, harp-guitars, harp-lyres, etc.

Sammlung alter Musikinstrumente, Kunsthistorisches Museum, Vienna (Schlosser Catalogue No. C. 67). Background: Oesterreichisches Museum für Angewandte Kunst, Vienna, T 8696 – Lemon-yellow Atlas silk, Italian, around 1700.

15 *"Gothic" Harp*

Italy, 16th century

The harp, one of the oldest stringed instruments, underwent many changes throughout its long history. Its basic shape in the Occident was determined by the relation of the three parts that form the frame: the sound box, whose walls are set into vibration by the strings; the curving neck which carries the tuning pins; and the pillar which helps to support the neck against the pull of the many strings. These three members were sometimes treated individually, that is, as quasi-independent parts of the whole—set off against each other by sculptured decoration at the joints. This was the case with the so-called "Romanesque" harp known to us chiefly from book illustration miniatures, and also with harps of the Baroque and Empire periods. In the Gothic period, however, the parts were fused into a slender, sleek, homogeneous frame, reflecting the prevailing style of other art forms in the twelfth and thirteenth centuries. It was this homogeneous frame that was, with minor changes, retained throughout the Renaissance and can be seen in the hands of angels in the pictures of Perugino and Raphael in the south, and of Dürer in the north.

The harp illustrated here is one of these "Gothic" harps. But one can clearly observe how a slight articulation of the pillar has set in under the impact of Italian sixteenth-century forms; on its front, the pillar carries an elegant scanthus pattern crowned by a mascherone.

Sammlung alter Musikinstrumente, Kunsthistorisches Museum, Vienna (Schlosser Catalogue No. C. 69).

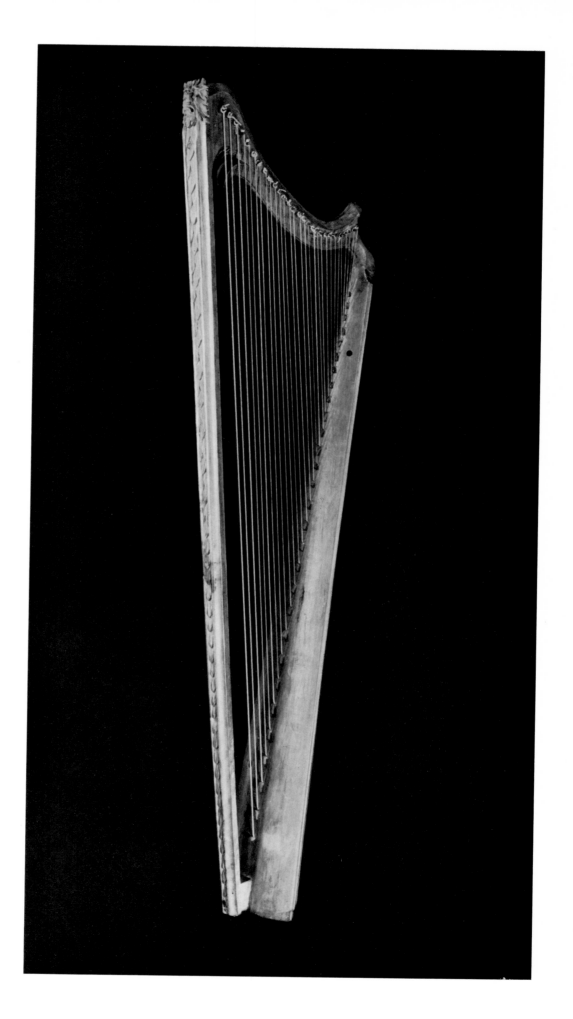

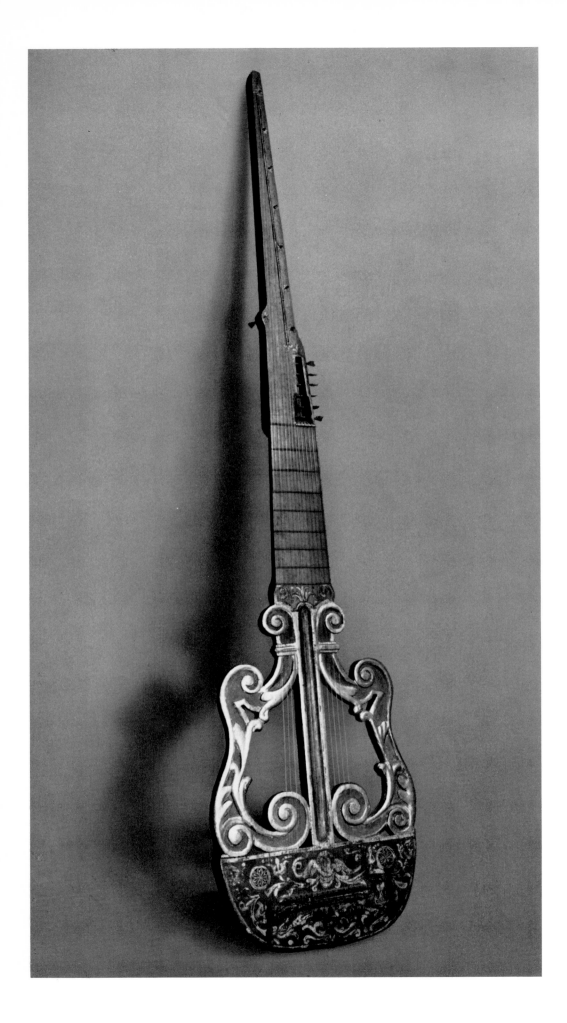

16   *Basslyre*

Italian, 16th century

This bizarre instrument consists of two quite different elements. One is an extremely flat sound box surmounted by a decorative structure of spirals, to suggest an ancient Greek lyre with its two arms. However, the arms carry no crossbar. The other part is simple and without decoration, but is functionally important: it is an extremely long neck with two pegboxes, precisely as we find it in the chitarrone (the long-necked bass lute of the late Renaissance and the Baroque). The lower pegbox on the right side serves a set of shorter strings – six in number; the upper pegbox serves the eight long bass strings.

The lyre part of the instrument, conspicuously painted in blue and gold, is so flat that no great sonority could have been expected from it. In all probability, the instrument was used in theatrical performances of ancient or pseudo-ancient plays or in scenes of mythological character. We can well imagine Orpheus or Apollo entering the stage and accompanying his recitation with an instrument of this kind, that posed as an ancient lyre but at the same time permitted at least some degree of actual musical performance.

Sammlung alter Musikinstrumente, Kunsthistorisches Museum, Vienna (Schlosser Catalogue No. A. 66).

17 *Set of five Tartölten*

Italian(?), 16th century

These five instruments, which seem to creep like fat snakes or dragons out of their box, are a set of unique wind instruments, the only specimens of their kind left by good fortune to posterity. An investigation of their inner structure reveals their use and function. They each conceal a metal tube consisting of nine or ten coils, which amounts to a remarkable acoustical length. The air enters from the player's mouth through the long thin tube which forms a twisted tail on the "dragon," and, after passing through the inner coils, comes out through the dragon's mouth with its trembling tongue.

Double bent tubes inside wind instruments were no rarity in the Renaissance – the modern bassoon is a last reminder of this shape. But there also existed many instruments with more complex inside coiling, for instance, the so-called "ranket" or "racket" (Wurst-fagott in German, and cervelat in French, because of its shape). Praetorius, in his famous *Organographia*, 1618, mentions and explains several families of reed instruments with inner coiling, such as the sorduns. There is no doubt that our five dragons were also reed instruments; they must have had double reeds, comparable to those of the modern bassoon, attached to the end of the metal crooks which form dragons' tails.

The name for these instruments – for they are listed in the Ambras inventory of 1596 – was Tartölden or Tartölten, a word not explained with certainty although it has been related to kortholt (kurzes Holz), a Renaissance precursor of the modern bassoon. The five sizes of our set are, in terms of range: two treble, two alto (or tenor) and one bass. They are made of brass and painted in bright, well-preserved colors. The flickering tongues are made of iron. The box is the one originally belonging to these instruments.

The question of how these instruments were used has also never been solved with certainty. It seems highly probable, however, that they were instruments for the theater, used with great effect on eye and ear in representations of certain exotic scenes: for instance, in representations of Hades, to accompany infernal demons; or for other allegorical or mythological purposes, such as visual and acoustical attributes of the characters of Jealousy or Envy. There are reports, to mention only one example, of feasts in Florence in 1565 where "four monstrous serpents" attacked four allegorical persons (Jealosy, Envy, Worry, and Spite), were taken hold of by them in defense, and suddenly revealed themselves as musical instruments.

Sammlung alter Musikinstrumente, Kunsthistorisches Museum, Vienna (Schlosser Catalogue No. C. 94). Background: Oesterreichisches Museum für Angewandte Kunst, Vienna, T 9060. – Section of a bed canopy, lemon-yellow Atlas silk, first half 18th century.

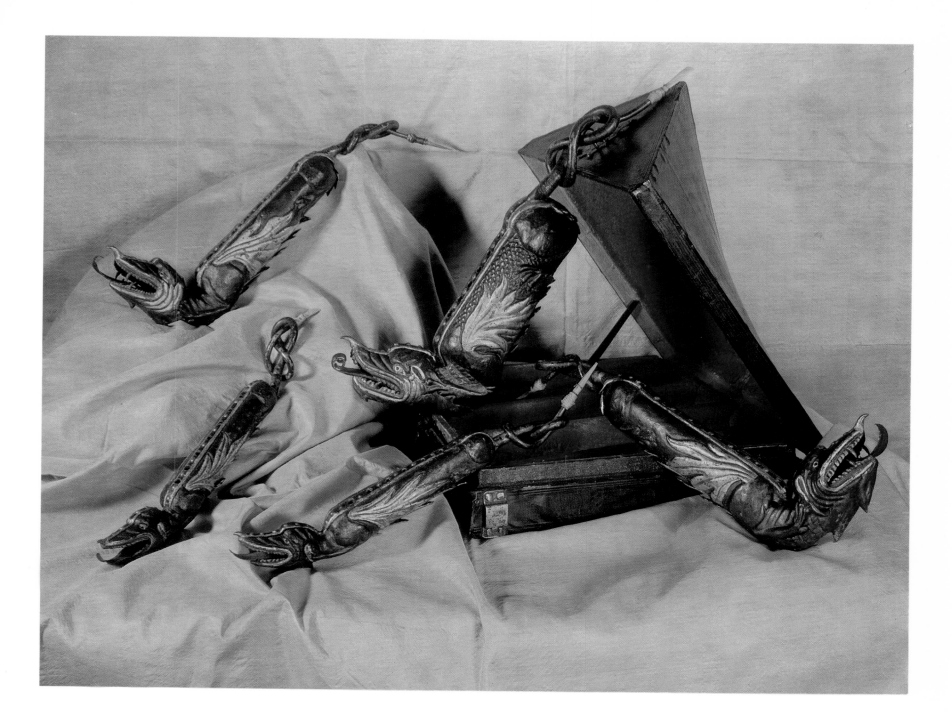

18 *Pochette in the form of a fish*

Italian, 16th century · Inscribed : "Baptista Bressano"

The sleek and slender form of the fish lends itself easily to some kinds of musical instruments. In the East – China and Japan – one of the important temple instruments originating during the Chou dynasty and used in the Taoistic and Buddhist cults is the "wooden fish," a slit drum in fish form, usually beautifully carved with many scales.

This pochette has the head of a dolphin, elaborate fins, and a tapering body encrusted with scales which decrease in size with the tapering. Especially ingenious is the elegantly coiled fishtail, which still manages to serve the function of a pegbox.

It seems quite possible that this instrument, along with the Tartölten and basslyre immediately preceding it on these pages, was built for use on the stage. One could imagine many aquatic topics, in intermedia and other spectacles, where such instruments might have been played or at least held by Amphion, Nereids, Tritons, or other mythological water creatures.

Museo Civico di Bologna – L. M. n. 16. (Catalogue No. 64 of "Mostra di Antichi Strumenti Musicali" by Luisa Cervelli, Comune di Modena, Teatro Comunale, 1963/64.)

19 *Viola da Gamba*

by John Rose in Bridewell, London, ca. 1590

From the middle of the sixteenth century until about 1640, the viol played a leading role in England, competing with the lute in the performance of subtle polyphonic music. As for English viol makers, we have the statement of Thomas Mace that there were "no better in the world."

The instrument here has a body of complex contour, composed of four undulating curves, sloping shoulders, and an unusual curvature of the tail end. The soundboard has flame holes and a decoration of widely spaced, brown arabesques. In the bridge section is the coat of arms of the Beaufort family, painted in intense colors. The side walls show a combination of incised, interlaced strapwork and Moresque design. The pegbox culminates in a finely carved female head.

John Rose, whose name is also found as "Ross" and "Rosa," was a celebrated instrument maker in London who was highly praised in Thomas Mace's *Musick's Monument* (London, 1676). Sir John Hawkins, in his famous *General History of the Science and Practice of Music* (London, 1776), credited him with the invention – "in the fourth year of Queen Elizabeth" – of the "Bandore," that is, the Pandora (see Pl. 43).

Oxford, Ashmolean Museum

20 *Spinettina*

Venice, 1540, made for Eleonora della Rovere
*Inscribed: "Ordinata e Fatta per Sua Eccelenza la Sig.*ra *Duchesa D'Urbino L'anno di Nostra*
Salute 1540 e pagata. 250 Scudi Romani"

The spinettina is only one of several keyboard instruments whose strings are plucked, either by quills cut from bird feathers or by leather plectra. Among the larger forms were the Italian spinetta and the French épinette, which probably derive their names from spina, meaning thorn or quill. The smallest form was the spinettina. It was made in many shapes, with trapezoid or pentagonal boxes. Most of the earlier forms had their wrest planks with the tuning pins at the right-hand end, and the strings stretched across the box, parallel to the keyboard, from right to left. The early history of quill instruments is still little known, but this spinettina is one of the earliest instruments extant of its kind.

This Venetian spinettina, acquired by the Metropolitan Museum of Art in recent years, is unique in several respects. It is miraculously preserved, as if it had left the workshop of its maker only yesterday, and is still in perfect playing condition. The decoration is unostentatious but of greatest refinement and elegance: a subtle combination of carving and intarsia. The keyboard projects out from the sound box, as in all Italian keyboard instruments of the time; it has thirty white and twenty black keys flanked by projecting side walls which are intricately carved and painted. On the rim of these walls sit a snake and another leaf-covered monster, combined. On the head of the monster is perched a winged female form with goat feet. Both sides of the walls are carved with twigs, leaves, and fruit designs. Beneath this design, on the outside of the walls, are painted golden spirals on a dark background. The frontboard has alternating squares, some in geometrical inlay of mother-of-pearl, *alla Certosina* (from the work of charterhouse monks), and some in wooden Gothic tracery on a blue background. To the left and right of the keyboard are two panels of stylized floral and leaf patterns in marquetry of maple, mahogany, and gum wood. Ivory buttons decorate the edges of the sound box and the partitions between the frontal intarsias and traceries. The jack rail and its buttons are made of layers of various woods. Near the front of the soundboard the sunken sound hole is of beautiful Gothic design.

Beneath the frontboard and immediately above the keys is a long strip of wood with the motto:

"Riccho son d'oro – et riccho son di suono,	*"I'm rich in gold and I am rich in sound,*
Non mi sonar si tu non ha del buono."	*O touch me not if no good tune is found."*

This whole strip can be removed, and on its back it bears the inscription, in Italian chancery of the time "Ordinata e Fatta per Sua Eccelenza la Sig.ra Duchesa D'Urbino L'anno di Nostra Salute 1540 e pagata. 250 Scudi Romani 33 (see title above).

Devotion to fine musical instruments was a tradition in the Este family. Eleonora della Rovere was the daughter of Isabella d'Este, who was an expert clavichord and lute player as well as a collector of instruments. Isabella kept jealous count of the precious instruments possessed by her sister Beatrice, at the Sforza court in Milan, with an eye to securing them at her sister's death. Among her profuse correspondence are many letters to Lorenzo Gugnasco da Pavia, her agent for procuring art treasures, curiosities, and musical instruments. Characteristically, Gugnasco was not only a dealer in art objects, but also a celebrated builder of outstanding musical instruments.

New York, Metropolitan Museum of Art, 53.6 (Pulitzer Bequest Fund, 1953).

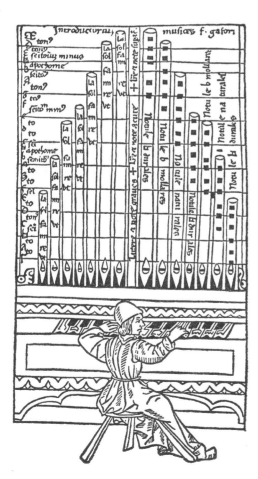

21 *Positive Organ*

Italian, around 1500

Only a few Italian positives of the sixteenth century survive. The present one excels by its unusually good state of preservation and its beautiful proportions.

There are three registers, all of open metal pipes: a four-foot, a two-foot, and a one-foot stop, but no wooden pipes. The keys are connected by wires with the wind chest.

The design of the organ, its noble proportions as well as the whole decorative scheme, is of great art-historical interest. The prospect, in triptych fashion, has three groups of pipes, set into separate arcades—the middle one much higher—and separated by thin columns. The very shallow reliefs above the pipe compartments, and those decorating the base and its plinth, are of exquisite design and show a fusion of Gothic with early Renaissance forms. Under the frieze we observe the coats of arms of the della Rovere family, with the oak tree, each flanked by two cornucopias and dolphins. The base is designed as an arcade or loggia of five niches, which are separated from each other by broad pilasters decorated with crude arabesques. In the three middle panels the story of Judith is represented; in the two flanking ones stand gadrooned vases from which palmettes emerge. The plinth of the base shows a frieze of similar but larger vases, enclosed in large oval frames of Gothic shape and connected by garlands.

The contrast between the shimmering pipe prospect and the softer tone of the gilded stucco reliefs, as well as the harmony between the upper and lower reliefs, make this organ a very remarkable piece of furniture.

Karl-Marx-Universität, Leipzig (Catalogue by Georg Kinsky, No. 241).

22 *Organ-Spinettino*

South German, 2nd half of the 16th century

This is one of the instruments – not at all rare in the late Renaissance and the Baroque – that tried to bring several different tone colors under the control of ten fingers acting on one keyboard. It combines the sound of plucked strings with that of wind instruments of two different tone colors: labial pipes (flue pipes) with a tone similar to that of recorders and reed pipes. The first are located at the rear of the box, and the latter are directly under the keyboard. On the two rectangular platforms at the left and right side of the keyboard, one can see buttons for the stops controlling the various registers.

The inventory of the famous Musaeum Septalianum of the Milanese nobleman Manfredo Settala, made in 1664, lists a similar instrument of Flemish origin, referring to it as a Proteus among the instruments ("ne proteus inter instrumenta desit...") because of its variety of sound.

The box of the instrument is painted in green with white and red flowers. The upper boards of the two bellows are decorated with intense colors, depicting grotesques in the Italian manner, including faces, satyrs, snakes, and flowers.

Sammlung alter Musikinstrumente, Kunsthistorisches Museum, Vienna (Schlosser Catalogue No. A. 132). Background: Oesterreichisches Museum für Angewandte Kunst, Vienna – T8696, Large, yellow-green Damask silk; Italian, c. 1700.

GLAVICIMBAL.

Wann Orgel und Regal zu starck beÿ Music chören
so diene ich vergnügt: des Clavicimbels Schall
läßt durch die Wunder-Faust auch Wunder dinge hören
es dringt durch Hertz und Ohr der angenehme Hall.
kommt eine schöne Fug und rare Phantasien
so muß was sonst betrübt in Augenblick öntfliehen.

23 *Harpsichord*

by Jerome of Bologna, 1521 · Inscribed: "HIERONYMUS BONONIENSIS FACIEBAT ROMAE MDXXI"

This instrument is one of the earliest dated harpsichords extant, if not actually the earliest. The frontboard, covered with gilt tooled leather, bears the inscription of the maker and, above that, the following distich: "Aspicite ut trahitur suavi modulamine vocis/Quicquid habent ser sidere terra fretum."

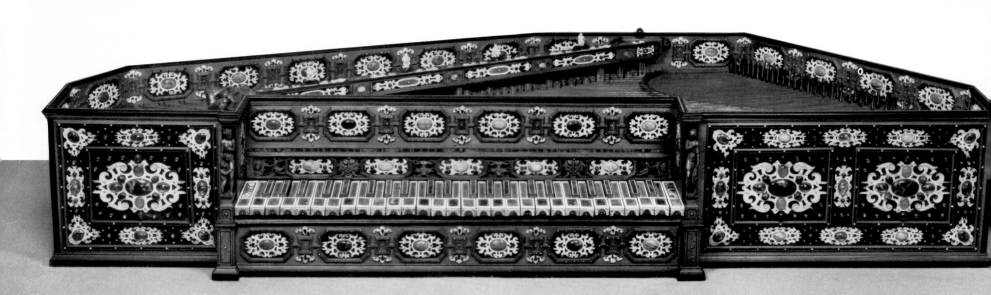

The harpsichord itself is made of cypress wood and, as was customary with Italian harpsichords, it is protected by an outer casing. Often the instruments themselves had little decoration except for the rose in the soundboard, while the outer cases were lavishly adorned. The case here, although certainly later than the instrument itself, is interesting because of its typical seventeenth-century decoration. The illustration shows the leather-covered front lid, leaning against the main lid at the upper left. The fronts of the keys are characteristically arcaded.

This instrument, which once had a pedal attachment like an organ, has undergone important structural changes.

London, Victoria and Albert Museum, No. 226–1879.

24 *Spinettino*

by Annibale Rossi, Milan, 1577 · Inscribed: "ANNIBALIS DE ROXIS MEDIOLANENSIS MDLXXVII"

This instrument is—if not the most beautiful—certainly the most costly keyboard instrument of the Renaissance extant, for it is studded with precious stones. The front walls flanking the keyboard and those above and beneath it are ornamented with strapwork panels carved in ivory on ebony ground, and each has several precious stones in the center. The wooden moldings surrounding the strapwork are set with garnets and turquoises. Lapis lazuli panels are set into the jack rail. There are also two small figures of a man in armour and a woman with a child, made of boxwood, standing on little pedestals that flank the keyboard. On top of the jackrail are four small ivory putti with musical instruments.

The Victoria and Albert Museum has made a count of the precious stones used: There are

857 turquoises	4 crystals	32 sapphires
103 lapis lazuli	52 jaspers	242 small garnets and rubies
58 topazes	361 pearls	9 agates, and
40 emeralds	28 amethysts	19 small jaspers and agates
117 garnets	6 carnelians	

a total of 1928 stones.

Four keyboard instruments by Annibale Rossi are known to exist today, the earliest dated 1550. The dates of his birth and death are unknown. Paolo Morigia in his very informative book on distinguished Milanese citizens, including artisans, gives Annibale Rossi great praise for the "rara bellezza e bontà" of his keyboard instruments and mentions a bejeweled instrument, probably the one illustrated here, in the possession of Carlo Trivulzio.

London, Victoria and Albert Museum, No. 809–1869.

25 *Double Virginal*

by Martin van der Biest, Antwerp, 1580 · Inscribed: "MARTINUS VAN DER BIEST M(E) F(ECIT) 1580"

This splendidly decorated instrument is the earliest double virginal known. Characteristic of its Flemish provenience is the oblong shape of the box, the receding keyboards, and the scheme of decoration, including block-printed paper, inset medallions, and elaborate paintings on the inside of the lid.

To the right of the fixed keyboard the large case accommodates a second and smaller instrument—the "ottavino." Normally it is placed in a drawer there, so that both keyboards appear side by side. But it can be removed and placed on top of the soundboard of the large instrument; in this position the jacks of the large instrument automatically lift those of the small one, so that each key of the lower keyboard operates on the strings of both instruments at the same time.

The two sections of the lid are decorated inside with excellent paintings. The larger, lower section shows a typical Garden of Love, a favorite subject of the time (of which an outstanding example is Rubens' picture now in the Prado Museum). A large fountain with the three Graces forms the center of the painting, amorous couples people the foreground, and in the background a banquet in an arbor is depicted. To the left of the garden scene, a wide vista opens upon a river bordered by peasants' huts, with a small castle in the distance. To the right a large and sumptuous castle, evidently an actual portrait, dominates the landscape. The narrower section of the lid, which protects the keyboards when the instrument is closed, shows the dramatic meeting of Saul and David, flanked at each side by groups of musical instruments. These paintings are of the seventeenth century.

The instrument is decorated with no less than seven portrait medallions, actually cast from pre-existing medals. They include Alexander Farnese; William of Nassau (William of Orange); Maximilian of Austria and his wife; Mary of Burgundy; Charlotte of Bourbon, Princess of Orange; King Philip II and his wife, Ann of Austria. It has been said that the instrument was made for Alexander Farnese, who was made governor-general of the Netherlands in 1578. But the gallery of nobles represented here in these medallions doesn't actually offer any clue as to whether the instrument was made for any one of them.

Antwerp, teeming in the sixteenth century with artistic life of every kind, was the home of many celebrated instrument makers. It is significant that these craftsmen belonged to the same guild as the painters: the famous Guild of St. Luke. Martin van der Biest entered this guild in 1557. During the Spanish occupation of the Lowlands there was a flourishing export of instruments, especially keyboard instruments, from Antwerp to Spain and also to the Spanish colonies.

Nuremberg, Germanisches Nationalmuseum, No. MI-85.

MVSICA · DVLCE · LABORVM · LEVAMEN

26 *Double Virginal*

by Hans Ruckers, Antwerp, 1581 · Inscribed: "HANS RVEKERS ME FECIT 1581"; *on string box:* "H. R." *and cipher in cartouche*

The basic construction of this double virginal is the same as that on the preceding plate except for the fact that here the small removable ottavina is on the left side. This instrument, which was formerly in the chapel of a country estate near Cuzco, Peru, came to the Metropolitan Museum of Art in damaged condition, with much of the wood inside the lid and the side walls eaten by borers. But fortunately the jack mechanism and the surface with its painting and other decorations were still intact, and the restoration work—fumigation and filling of cavities with plastic wood—was successful. Only the jack rail of the main instrument was replaced—by a copy made like the rail of the ottavina.

When closed, the instrument resembles a black coffin. But the inside is lavishly decorated: the soundboard, painted with fruits, flowers, and a bird, has two gilded roses of geometric design; the side walls show an elaborate wallpaper design but, unlike many other Flemish keyboard instruments which have actual wallpaper glued on, it is painted. The little box for strings and the tuning key on the left front corner of the main instrument bear the initials of Hans Ruckers and his ciphers in an escutcheon. The dropboard, as was customary, bears a Latin motto: "MUSICA · DULCE · LABORUM · LEVAMEN."

The two medallions above the keyboard of the larger instrument are of gilded gesso and cast from bronze medals of the time. The right one represents Philip II of Spain (inscribed "PHILLIPPUS HISPANIAE ET NOVI ORBIS OCCIDUI REX"); the left one shows the fourth wife of Philip II, Anne of Austria (inscribed "ANNA AUSTRIACA, PHILYPPI CATHOL"). As the queen died in 1580, one may assume that the instrument was commissioned before that time.

The lid for the protection of the keyboards is not connected with the main instrument, as it is in the double virginal by van der Biest; here it is attached with hinges beneath the keyboards, to be turned up when the instrument was closed. This arrangement is more pleasing, because here there is no conflict with the painting on the upper lid. Although there are many similarities between the lid paintings of the two instruments, there is a principal difference in the layout of the landscape. Here it is a wide, flat terrace rather than a garden, separated by railings from the background. On the left, some steps lead toward the river and a waiting boat. On the extreme right is a playground for the game of pall-mall, and behind it an oblong arbor. At the left behind the boat is a castle complete with steeples and a drawbridge. Glancing over the landscape, the eye can detect many delightful details, such as a game preserve with several deer and a black bear, a windmill, and countless courtiers enjoying the out-of-doors.

Of special interest are the many musical instruments. At the banquet in the center, two people play the lute. On the steps of the central pavillion we observe: at the left, another lute, a cornetto, a flute, and a music book; on the right, an open lute case, a shawm, and two pipes. Still further to the right is a little band, consisting of two shawms and one cromorne (Krummhorn), providing music for the dance.

Hans Ruckers the Elder was the founder of the most famous Flemish dynasty of makers of keyboard instruments. In 1575 he was admitted to the Guild of St. Luke, as a *Claversinbalmakerre*. The discovery of an instrument of his in Peru makes it probable that the flourishing export of Netherlandish keyboard instruments reached also to the Spanish possessions in the New World.

New York, Metropolitan Museum of Art. 29.90. Gift of B. H. Homan, 1929.

27 *Trumpet in D*

Marked on bell rim in raised gilded letters:
"MACHT ANTON SCHNITZER NUREMBERG A. MDLXXXI" *(1581)*

This fanfare trumpet is one of the most exquisitely decorated instruments which has come out of that celebrated center of brass instrument making, Nuremberg. It is made of silver. The "garland" round the bell, the sleeves at the joints, and the mouthpiece are decorated with gilded "garnishes", and so is the "boss" (or "ball") in the middle of the bell branch.

The whole tube except for the wider part near the bell is engraved with a fine scalelike pattern. The wide part has more elaborate foliate ornamentation, and near the bell there are four allegorical female figures standing in arcades and holding musical instruments: cornetto, trombone, lute, and harp. The two small metal loops inside the upper and lower bend held the pennant.

Since the mouthpiece has the same golden ornamentation as other parts of the instrument, it must be considered as the one originally made for this trumpet. Mouthpieces are easily detachable and therefore often lost; and any keeper of a collection of instruments knows from bitter experience how rare "authentic" mouthpieces are. Yet they are priceless evidence of the tonal capacity of an instrument, permitting valuable conclusions as to its range and timbre. The mouthcup of our trumpet has the broad flat rim and, inside, the sharp-edged "throat" that facilitated easy playing in the high register.

Anton Schnitzer belonged to a celebrated family of brass instrument makers in Nuremberg; several beautiful examples of his craft survive in European collections.

Sammlung alter Musikinstrumente, Kunsthistorisches Museum, Vienna (Catalogue by Julius von Schlosser, No. A. 258). Background: Oesterreichisches Museum für Angewandte Kunst, Vienna, T. 9054 – Part of the canopy of a four-poster bed; dark blue damask, first half of 18th century; from the Schloßhof; T 2910 – Red silk with gold pattern, Venice, mid-15th century.

28 *Trumpet in E flat*

by Anton Schnitzer, Nuremberg, 1598
Marked: "MACHT ANTONI SCHNITZER IN NVRMBERG 1598"

During its long history, the trumpet assumed various shapes. Its earliest from, as far as we can learn from pictures of the Middle Ages, was a straight tube of not more than about five feet in length. Later, when the scale was expanded, the tube was made longer and had to be bent in order to be manageable for the player. In pictures from the thirteenth and fourteenth centuries, we find trumpets bent in S shape side-by-side with the older, straight form. Still later the curves of the S were flattened into three parallel sections of tube connected by U bends.

Other ways of bending and coiling were occasionally tried. One was circular coiling in horn fashion; another is the one adopted for the instrument shown here – a coiling in pretzel shape, composed of a large figure eight, with two small perfect circles at the sides. The length of the whole tube is no less than 208 cm, and compared with this the width of the bell appears unusually small (10 cm). This instrument of gilded brass is, like the preceding trumpet, from the famous workshop of Anton Schnitzer in Nuremberg.

Kunsthistorisches Museum, Vienna. Property of the Gesellschaft der Musikfreunde, No. 181 (inventory of the collection by E. Mandyczewski).

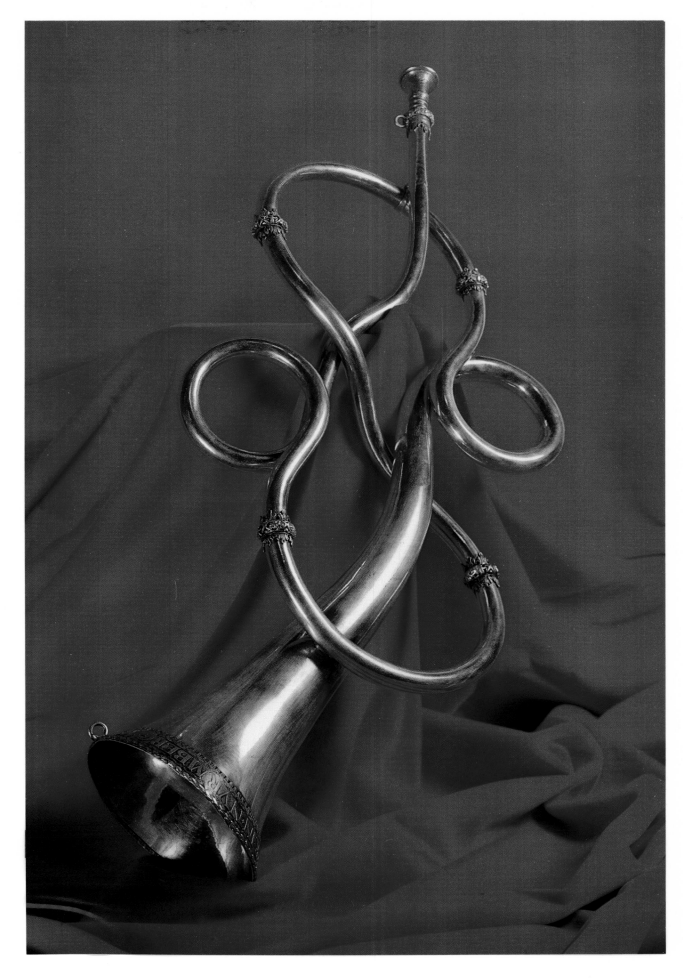

29 *Organ in St. Giovanni in Laterano, Rome*

built by Luca Blasi, 1597–1600
Carvings and other decorations by Giovanni Battista Montani

This Plate and Plate 85 show two large church organs. Two examples are of course a pitifully small number to suggest the complexity and variety of problems involved in the long history of the queen of instruments, and especially the change of its visual aspects. But a comparison of a characteristic instrument of the late Renaissance with one of the late Baroque may, at least, suggest to the eye the degree of change that took place within a span of only 150 years.

The large organ in the basilica of San Giovanni in Laterano – "the cathedral of Rome and the world" – is located at the rear wall of the right arm of the transept. It was commissioned by Clemens VIII (Aldobrandini) and is one of the largest in Rome. Its immediate architectural surroundings are in the late Renaissance style, and it was built of course to harmonize with this environment. Its basic design is that of the Classical triumphal arch. The middle pediment is supported by a pair of large Corinthian columns, and the arch inside by a pair of pilasters. The two side sections are each flanked by smaller columns. This tripartite scheme is filled in by nine compartments of pipes, three in each of the openings of the triumphal arch and three in each side section, always with the longest pipes in the center.

Each of these sections forms a flat surface, and together they make a back wall that harmonizes with the windows of the side wall and the coffered ceiling. Thus, with all its splendor, the organ forms a natural, classical, static backdrop, completely absorbed as it were by the language of the forms surrounding it in the cathedral.

The beautiful carved decoration was executed by Giovanni Battista Montani, a native-born Milanese who worked for many years in Milan as an architect, woodcarver, and goldsmith until, like many other Lombards, he was called to Rome (under the Pontificate of Gregory XIII), where he became a member of the celebrated Congregazione dei Virtuosi. Among the statues adorning the organ are those of God the Father, on top of the middle arch, and the Virgin Mary and the Angel of the Annunciation on top of the two side sections. Each of the subsections of the central compartment is embellished by a musical angel; and beneath the central angel, a horizontal ledge bears a quotation from Psalm 150: "LAUDATE DEUM IN CHORDIS ET ORGANO."

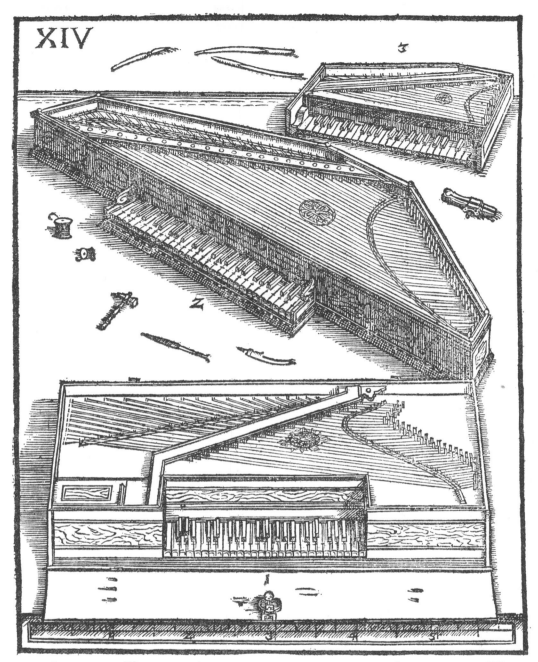

I. 2. Spinetten: Virginal (ingemein Instrument genant) so recht Chor-Thon.
3. OctavInstrumentlin.

30 *Spinettina*

Augsburg (?), 17th century

The decoration of this colorful and attractive instrument is an outstanding example of South German late Renaissance design. The basic shape of the instrument, with its receding keyboard, still follows the traditional Flemish pattern. In the same tradition is the use of the Latin motto on the jack rail – "sic transit gloria mundi" – and other embellishments: the use of bone

32 *Clavicytherium*

Italian, early 17th century

"Clavicytherium" was the old name for the upright harpsichord; it was used as early as 1511 in Sebastian Virdung's *Musica getutscht* ("Treatise on Music in *Deutsch*"). The upright form of the harpsichord entailed technical difficulties which did not occur in the normal, horizontal form of the instrument. In the latter, the wooden jacks, equipped with little quills which pluck the strings, fall back by their own weight as soon as the player releases the key. In the upright harpsichord, the jacks move horizontally and must therefore be brought back into their resting position by a special device using a metal spring. This delicate mechanism was expensive. But on the other hand, a vertical soundboard had advantages: it projected the sound directly toward the listener, and also it saved space, just as the upright piano does today. Usually these instruments had an unadorned, wing-shaped soundboard towering over the keyboard. In this clavicytherium, the vertical plane was used as a basis for an extensive painting display. The soundboard fills part of an oblong case which has folding doors decorated inside and out with representations of musicians—a singer and instrumentalists. The instruments on the inside of the doors are: cornetto, treble viol, and bass viol. On the outside (not visible here) are representations of a lute, a transverse flute, a trombone, and a harp.

The largest and at the same time most imaginative painting is found in the space in the rectangular central box, left open because of the trapezoidal shape of the soundboard. Here, King David plays his harp, and it was a witty idea of the painter to have this harp nestling in the concave curve of the soundboard of the harpsichord, so that King David almost appears to play the strings of the latter. And, in fact, his harp is actually placed in an unplayable position, with the pillar next to King David so that its sound chest, instead of leaning against the shoulder of the player, fits against the curve of the harpsichord soundboard (a curve which, like that of the harp, is determined by the gradation of the strings).

New York, Metropolitan Museum of Art, 89.4.1224 (Crosby Brown Collection, 1889).

33 *Geigenwerk*

by Fray Raymundo Truchado, 1625
(keyboard instrument with four friction wheels)
Inscribed, "FRAY RAYMUNDO TRUCHADO · INVENTOR · 1625"

This ingenious instrument was supposed to produce the sound of a whole ensemble of bowed instruments through the fingers of a single player acting on the keyboard. The forty-five gut strings are stretched over a soundboard and set into vibration by the rims of four rotating steel wheels that are inserted into the soundboard. Each of the rims, covered with a band of cloth, acts like an unending bow. Wire loops at the ends of the keys serve to pull the strings down against the rims of the friction wheels. The wheels are controlled by means of a hidden master wheel that is turned by a crank at the rear of the instrument. Thus, as in the organ and harpsichord, up to ten tones could be sounded simultaneously, producing a rich polyphony like that of a whole consort of viols. An additional advantage not inherent in the organ or harpsichord of the time was the possibility of modifying the finger pressure and thus the tone volume, as in a clavichord or in the pianoforte, a century later.

In spite of signing as "inventor", Truchado was not the first to build such an instrument. Actually this instrument is only a free imitation of one invented half a century earlier by Hans Hayden in Nuremberg, and described with admiration and in great detail by Michael Praetorius in his *Syntagma Musicum* of 1618, where it is called the "Nurnbergisch Geigenwerck." Hayden built several models, one of them operating by means of a long revolving belt serving as an "unending bow" rather than with wheels.

But even Hayden was not the first to think of such an instrument. More than a century before his invention, Leonardo da Vinci drew a number of different blueprints for a "viola organista" on pages in the *Codex Atlanticus*, Ambrosiana, Milan, and the *Manuscript H*, Institut Français, Paris; and as these sketches reveal, he also experimented with various friction devices: a rotating belt as an unending bow, and also a friction wheel.[6] However, we have no way of knowing whether Leonardo actually built such instruments, and it is extremely unlikely that Hayden knew of Leonardo's experiments.

The lid of our instrument here bears the main decoration: the oblong section shows a woman being abducted by two fishtailed Tritons, while above her hovers a flying cupid; the sloping section carries an architectural scenario in deep perspective. The latter was evidently cut down from a perfectly symmetrical painting in order to fit the lid. At any rate, the two paintings are so different in style and subject that one is tempted to assume that they were not originally intended for the instrument.

Brussels, Instrument Museum of the Royal Conservatory of Music, Cat. 2485.

Nůrmbergisch Gei-
genwerck.

III

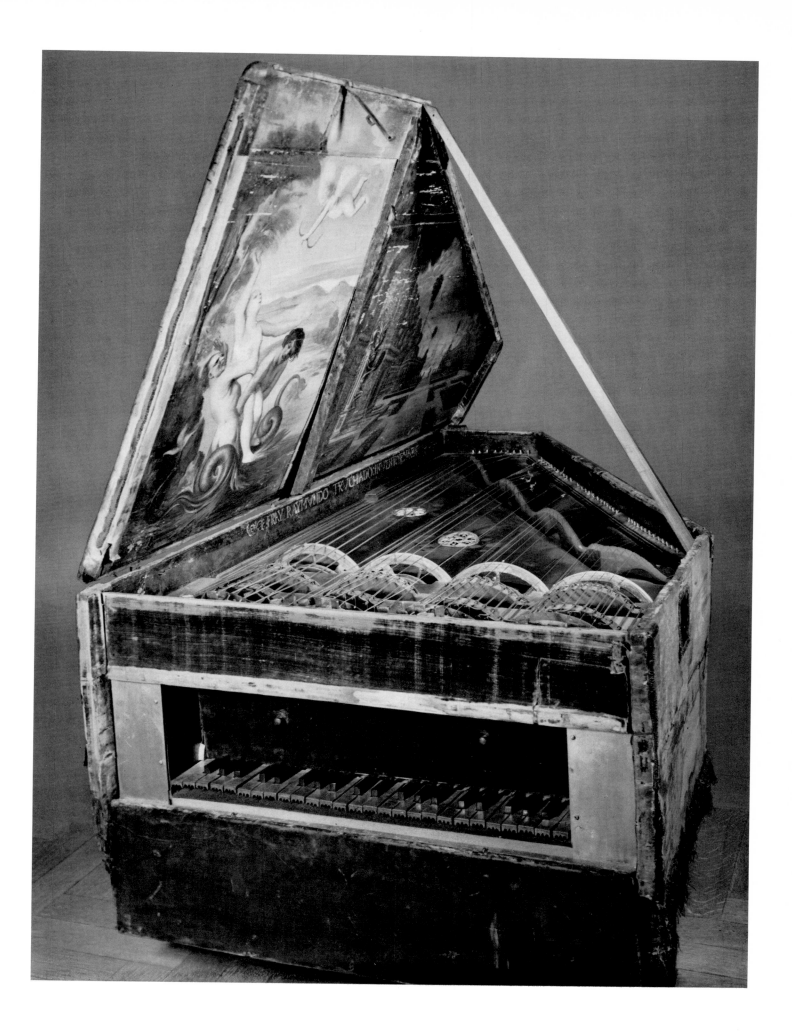

34 *Harpsichord*

by Hans Ruckers, the Younger, Antwerp, 1627
Inscribed on the frontboard: "JOHANNES RUCKERS FECIT ANTVERPIAE"

The maker of this instrument was the second son of Hans Ruckers, the maker of the double virginal illustrated on Pl. 26. The instrument is dated on the soundboard. It has one manual and two four-foot sets of strings. Unlike Italian harpsichords, there is no outer case.

The inside of the lid shows a coastal landscape and, above, one of the mottoes customary on Flemish keyboard instruments: "*Musica Donum Dei.*" The beautiful rose in the soundboard has the usual design showing a harp-playing angel flanked by the maker's initials, J R. The front slats of the lower keys are gilded; the upper keys are dark-stained oak.

Berlin, Staatliche Musikinstrumentensammlung (Catalogue by Curt Sachs, No. 2227).

35 *Octave Spinet*

South German, 2nd quarter of the 17th century

This small and graceful instrument, only 45 cm in length, is a good example of the frequent combination of a small keyboard instrument with a sewing box. The latter purpose may even have been the more important one in this case, for the keys are extremely narrow and the pitch very high. Possibly it was meant for a children's instrument.

The case is of ebony, decorated with applied silver ornamentation typical of South German workmanship. There are several circular and oval medallions set in, all embellished with etching, engraving, and enameling. The style of all this decoration points to Augsburg or Munich, where it was traditional. The lid, decorated with a mirror, contains a box which opens by means of a sliding panel; and a drawer with a secret catch is contained in the base of the instrument.

London, Victoria and Albert Museum, No. 4265–1857.

36 *Harpsichord*

by Girolamo Zenti, Rome, 1658
Inscribed: "HIERONYMUS DE ZENTIS VITERBIENSIS. F(ecit) ROMAE ANNO DOM. MDCLVIII"

This instrument, typical in its functional construction of mid-seventeenth century Italian harpsichords, is made of cedar wood and has one manual acting on two sets of eight-foot strings. The soundboard is decorated with a large carved rose in flamboyant Gothic design. The legs are late additions.

The most outstanding feature of this harpsichord is its decoration of exquisite and well-preserved paintings that cover both sides of the lid and the side walls. The inside of the lid shows a Roman *campagna* landscape, a shepherd and animals in the foreground shade and a wide vista of mountains and sun-soaked horizon. The outside of the lid has a similar painting, but somewhat yellowed by its location. One can think of no better place to preserve a painting than on the inner side of a harpsichord lid, where it rests most of the time, surface down, in a closed box protected from dust and dirt. Every collector knows how fresh and intense the colors of inside paintings remain compared with those on the outer surface of the lid. The present instrument is a good example.

The painting on the side walls shows groups of animated putti connected by festoons and masks. Only the putti on the small end of the instrument (not visible here) were restored; they appear Victorian.

Girolamo Zenti's instruments must have been very much in demand. Born in Viterbo near Rome, he worked for Roman patrons. About 1668 we find him to be harpsichord maker to Charles II of England. Later he worked in Paris, and finally in Florence for Prince Ferdinand de' Medici. The inventory signed by Bartolommeo Cristofori in 1716, when he was made keeper of the Medici collection of musical instruments, includes no less than four instruments made by Zenti.

New York, Metropolitan Museum of Art, 89.4.1221 (Crosby Brown Collection, 1889).

37 *Harpsichord*

About 1650
Signed: "JOANNES COUCHET FECIT ANTWERP"

Jan Couchet was a nephew of Hans Ruckers the Elder (see Pl. 26) and continued the Ruckers tradition in Antwerp. In 1642 he entered the Guild of St. Luke. It is indicative of the quality of his instruments that he made harpsichords for Chambonnière, the harpsichordist at the court of Louis XIV, and that according to contemporary reports Chambonnière was very pleased by them.

Couchet transformed the earlier type of harpsichord into an instrument with three sets of strings and two keyboards, thus greatly expanding the number of possible combinations of volume and tone color and creating an ideal vehicle for Baroque polyphony.

The present instrument is a splendid example of Jan Couchet's workmanship. The decoration is in Louis XIV style: the outside of the case is painted with strapwork on gold ground; the bordered cartouches in gray enclose acanthus scrolls, shell forms, and pairs of cornucopia – like foliage sheaths supporting nosegays of spring flowers. Its inside walls are decorated by delicate arabesques of black foliate scrolls on gold ground; the stand and the legs originally made for this instrument are decorated in the same style.

New York, Metropolitan Museum of Art, 89.4.2363 (Crosby Brown Collection, 1889).

Der Organist.

Das Positiff mit süssem hal/
Schlag ich auff Bürgerlichem Sal/
Da die ehrbarn der Gschlecht sind gsessn/
Ein köstlich Hochzeitmal zu essen/
Daß jn die weil nicht werd zu lang
Brauchn wir die Leyern mit gesang/
Daß sich darvon jr Hertz eben/
In freud vnd wunne thu erhebn.

38 **Positive Organ**

Germany, 17th century

"Positive" was the traditional name for an organ that, although not a firm part of a church interior, was larger and heavier than the "portative" organ which could easily be carried around in processions. But the line of distinction is in many cases somewhat blurred.

The problem of the conflict between visual symmetry and acoustic necessity – that the length of pipes diminish from bass to treble – is solved very simply in our specimen: symmetry is abandoned, and the triangular space left open by the diagonal line formed by the upper ends of the pipes is filled with open scrollwork and the coat of arms and medallion portrait of Johann Georg I, Duke of Saxony (presumptuously shown as held by angels). The builder of the instrument was probably Gottfried Fritzsche, organ maker to the electoral court of Saxony.

The inner sides of the doors have tempera paintings representing the dismissal of Hagar (left) and the sacrifice by Abraham (right).

London, Victoria and Albert Museum, No. 2–1867.

39 *Harp*

Italy, about 1625

This monumental harp, the so-called *Arpa Barberini*, is a perfect example of the role of decoration in the vibrating and in the nonvibrating parts of a stringed instrument. The massive, pyramid-shaped sound box is virtually devoid of ornamentation. The pillar, however, and the joint between the neck and the sound box are laden with heavy carved decoration. The pillar – similar to candlesticks of the Roman Baroque – is actually transformed into a three-story edifice, supporting the coat of arms of the Barberini family. The upper story has a pair of putti wearing lions' skins, reminiscent of Hercules. The middle tier has angels very close in style to the stucco angels in the apse of S. Andrea della Valle, a church famous for the frescoes of Lanfranco and Domenichino, who worked there around 1625.[7] Urban VIII of the Barberini family was elected pope in 1624, and it stands to reason that an extravagant piece such as the *Arpa Barberini* was commissioned shortly after that event.

The *Arpa Barberini* plays a dominant role in one of the most charming paintings of Lanfranco, his "Allegory of Music," today in the Galleria Nazionale d'Arte Antica in the Palazzo Barberini, in Rome.[8] There a half-nude "Musica" plays this harp, which is precisely depicted in all its details and appears so overpowering that it almost becomes the protagonist of the picture.

Property of Principessa Henriette Barberini, Rome.

40 *Lute*

Italian (probably), first half of the 17th century

This lute has the typical pear shape characteristic of the instrument. From the fifteenth to the seventeenth century, the lute underwent a gradual change: it grew in size and the neck became wider to accommodate a larger number of strings. At the same time, a variety of outlines—sometimes apple shape (especially in Lombardy), sometimes pear shape—became the rule. With the widening of the neck, the esthetic problem of joining neck and body entered a new phase. In the earlier, thin-necked lutes, the body gradually continued into the neck from the point where the body narrowed at the top. But with the later lutes, the broad neck is strongly set off against the top of the bulging back, and the decorative scheme forcefully accentuates the contrast between the plane and the spherical element.

In this lute, the back is composed of nine ivory ribs with thin ebony spacers at their junctures. It contrasts strongly in color with the dark decoration of the neck, with its arabesque scrollwork in ebony on an ivory background. The decoration of the neck continues on the back-bent head; only the ivory pegs repeat the shimmering white of the vaulted back. The pine soundboard of this instrument (not shown) shows a carved rose, and the finger board is of plain ebony; eleven courses of strings, a single treble and ten double strings, are accommodated on the instrument.

London, Victoria and Albert Museum, No. 1125–1869.

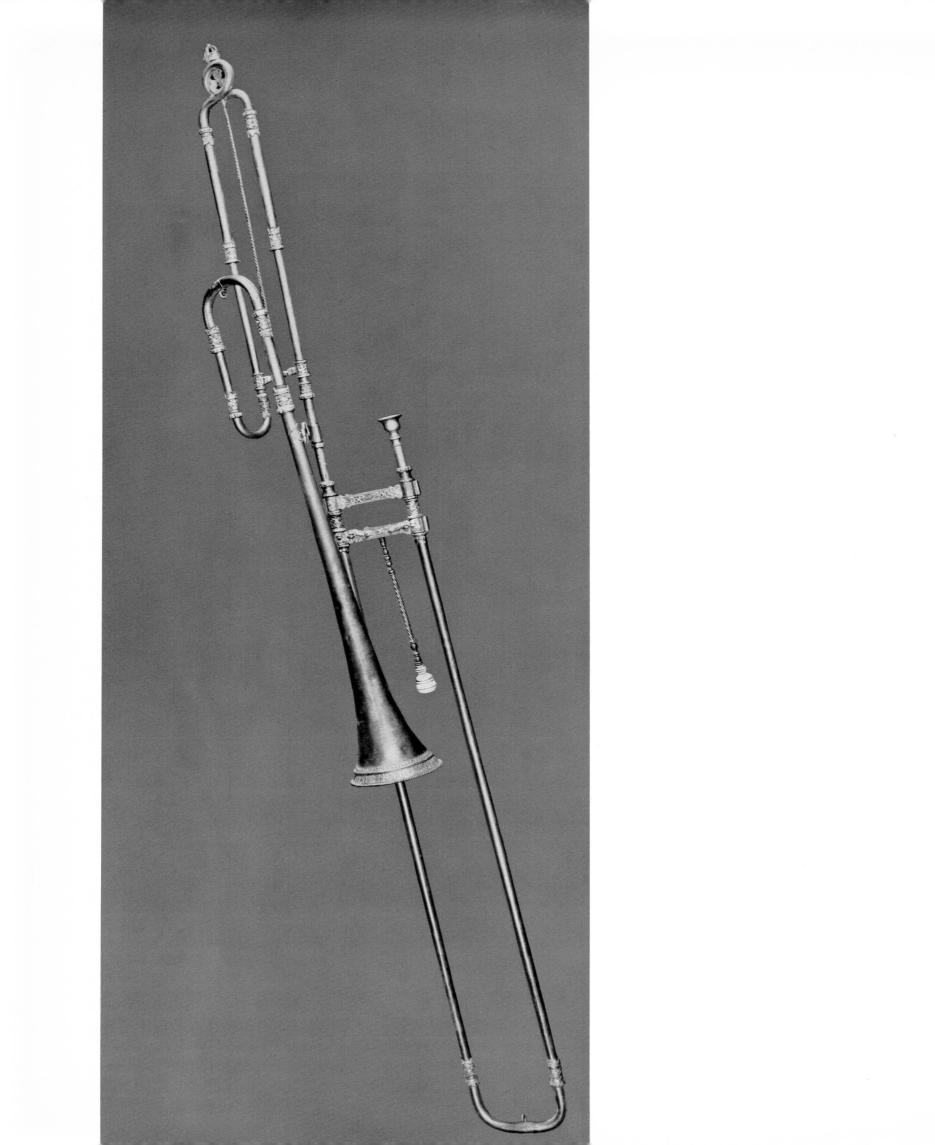

41 *Quintbass-Trombone*

by Johann Isaac Ehe, Nuremberg, 1612

A Quintbass-trombone (or simply Quint-trombone) is a trombone sounding one fifth lower than the tenor trombone and one octave lower than the alto trombone. By "trombone" we mean here the slide trombone, the most perfect and simple solution of a tricky problem, the shortening of the tube to achieve an unbroken chromatic scale on a brass instrument. We do not know who invented the telescopelike slide, nor when and where it was invented. But there is some good evidence for assuming that the slide was used as early as the fourteenth century.

Though this basic mechanism remained virtually unchanged throughout the ages, the tone color expected from the trombone changed considerably during its history. While in Mozart's and Wagner's orchestra it was to produce a majestic, overpowering, and sometimes even threatening effect, it was used for more suave and mellow tone in the Baroque period and before, when it blended well with string instruments, recorders, and the human voice.

The illustrated instrument is the earliest known specimen of a Quint-trombone, outstanding because of its fine workmanship and elegant proportions. It has already a swivel extention handle for shifting the slide in the lower positions.

Johann Isaac Ehe was an early member of a long dynasty of makers of brass instruments in Nuremberg, the leading center of the production of such instruments since the fifteenth century.

Germanisches Nationalmuseum, Nuremberg, No. M I 168.

42 *Viole da gamba (discant, alto, and tenor)*

Inscribed : "Antonio Ciciliano", Venice, 17th Century

Viole da gamba were among the most important string instruments from the sixteenth to the eighteenth century. They were highly esteemed for their noble, soft, and silvery timbre and their eminent usefulness for the performance of polyphonic music. The main characteristics of these instruments were their deep body with sloping shoulders, and their large number of strings (five to seven, usually six) which ran over a slightly arched bridge and were stopped with the help of frets. Viole da gamba were built in sets of several members, the whole family reaching from the violetta piccola down to instruments of double bass size. The present group comprises three instruments of different sizes: discant, alto, and tenor, all of similar shape and decoration and each with six strings.

Antonio Ciciliano, probably Bolognese by birth, worked in Venice in the first half of the seventeenth century, although his name – dialect for "Siciliano" – points to Sicily. Besides viols, he made lutes, chitarroni, and theorbos.

Vienna, Sammlung alter Musikinstrumente, Kunsthistorisches Museum (Catalogue by Julius Schlosser, 75, 76, 77). Background: Österreichisches Museum für Angewandte Kunst, Vienna, T 8696, yellow-green Damask, Italy about 1700.

43 *Pandora*

Italy, 17th century

During the sixteenth century there developed out of the family of citterns—with their flat front and back, lateral pegs, and wire strings—large varieties of instruments which differed in shape and other details, and became fashionable for about a century, especially in England. They had fancy names such as Pandora (bandora, bandoer), Orpheoreon (Orpharion), and Penorcon. They were chiefly used for accompanying the solo voice and as a bass continuo instrument in the ensemble. Not the least of their advantages was their sturdiness, especially in comparison with the lute, whose thin, bulging back required constant repairs.

According to tradition, the Pandora was invented in 1560 by the London instrument maker John Rose. It had an extravagant outline with three "swellings" of the edge and side walls. The instrument here, with the remarkable length of 121 cm, has a beautiful rose of geometrical design, sidewalls made of strips of hardwood separated by inlaid lines of maple, and a carved, bearded head on top of the curving pegbox. The finger board is made of hardwood stained dark.

New York, Metropolitan Museum of Art, 89.4.1021 (Crosby Brown Collection, 1889).

44 *Orpheoreon*

England, 1617 · Printed label: "Francis/Palmer/Dwelling in ... 1617"

Instruments such as this, with the suggestive name derived from Orpheus, were relatively rare. They are small relatives of the Pandora and, like the latter, were used primarily in England. The Pandora (Bandoer), Orpheoreon, and another similar instrument, the Penorcon, were all functionally derived from the bass cittern but characterized by their complex, many-curved outline.

Praetorius, in his *Organographia* (1618), devotes three chapters to the description of these instruments, whose cradle he believes to have been in England.

Copenhagen, Carl Claudius' Samling af Gamle Musikinstrumenter, Catalogue No. 139.

45 *Chitarra Battente*

by Matteo Sellas, Venice, ca. 1630. Inscribed (on a small ivory plaque at the pegboard):
"Matteo Sellas alla Corona in Venetia"

Chitarra Battente

by Giovanni Smit, Milan, 1646

Although we call both of these instruments *chitarra battente*, the one in the foreground, by Matteo Sellas, actually combines features of the guitar as well. The vaulted back is characteristic of the chitarra battente; the regular guitar had a flat back. On the other hand, the belly of the chitarra battente normally had a slope below the bridge, and the strings of metal were fastened to the very bottom of the instrument—actually to the ribs beneath the lower end of the soundboard. Sellas's instrument, however, has the flat soundboard of the guitar, and the gut strings are fastened to a frontal string holder. The soundboard is profusely decorated on its upper and lower parts by foliate scrolls in black wood, and is perforated by a circular sound hole with the traditional rose of stiff paper. The finger board is inlaid with ivory plaques engraved with Italian landscape scenes. Matteo Sellas is regarded as the most important Venetian lute maker, with the exception of Magnus Tieffenbrucker, who has been thought to be Sellas's teacher. Besides lutes and guitars, Sellas built chitarroni, theorbos, mandolas, and pandurinas.

The smaller instrument shows its characteristic curved back, composed of ebony ribs separated by ivory strips. The back of the neck has a checkerboard and arabesque design in black and white.

Both instruments come from the castle Catajo, near Padua, where since the seventeenth century the family Obizzi had accumulated a collection of art treasures which later came into the possession of the Habsburg dynasty.

The musical still life in the background is by the Bergamasque painter Bartolomeo Bettera, 1600.

Gemäldegalerie des Kunsthistorischen Museums, Vienna, No. 6990. Sammlung alter Musikinstrumente, Kunsthistorisches Museum, Vienna (Schlosser Cat. Nr. C. 51 and C. 52).

46 *Guitar*

Venice, 17th century

This is one of the most elegant guitars extant, made of ebony – except for the soundboard – and inlaid with Renaissance ornaments in ivory and inserted patterns of mother-of-pearl. Its back (not shown) is composed of eleven staves. The tail end of the soundboard is inlaid with three plaques of mother-of-pearl, the middle one of triangular, the two flanking ones of circular design. The same alternation between triangular and curved shapes recurs in the border of the beautiful sunken rose of Gothic design. The edge of the soundboard is made of black putty into which small pieces of mother-of-pearl have been set.

Karl-Marx-Universität, Leipzig (Catalogue by Georg Kinsky, No. 536).

47 *Double Guitar*

by Alexandre Voboam, Paris, 1690 · Signed: "ALEXANDRE VOBOAM 1690 PARIS", *on two little ivory plaques inserted into the pegboard*

Of these two guitars, joined together like Siamese twins, the larger is of standard size, 95 cm from top to bottom; the smaller is only 63.05 cm long, providing for a tuning about a third higher than that of the larger. Each of the instruments has five double strings, ten movable frets, and beautiful sunken gilded roses with shamrock patterns.

Alexandre Voboam was a well-known maker of guitars in Paris in the second half of the seventeenth century. Twin constructions like this one are of great rarity. The inventory of the famous Musaeum Septalianum, founded by the Milanese nobleman Manfredo Settala in the seventeenth century, mentions under No. 40 a Spanish double guitar ("chitharae duae ex uno corpore resultantes Hispaniis editae").

Vienna, Sammlung alter Musikinstrumente, Kunsthistorisches Museum (Catalogue by Julius von Schlosser, No. 57).

48 *Chitarra Battente*   *Guitar*   *Chitarra Battente*

Italian, 18th century   *French, 18th century*   *Italian, ca. 1700*

The guitar derives its name (gittern, guitare, guiterne, chitarra, guitara) from the ancient ϰιϑάρα (kithara). In the ancient Greek instrument, of course, the strings ran freely from the sound box to the crossbar, and there was no finger board against which to stop them. The strings of the guitar, like that of the lute, mandolin, and most bowed instruments of the Occident, can be stopped against the long finger board. Characteristic of the guitar is its flat body with elegantly incurved side walls and a round (often open) sound hole, a long fretted neck, and a flat pegboard with the pegs inserted from the rear. The gut strings of the guitar are plucked by the fingers, without a plectrum. The back of the guitar shown here (at the right) has a fascinating inlaid design of cubes in *trompe l'œil*. Inlaid strips of ebony decorate the side walls; and the soundboard, neck, and head are also inlaid with ebony, in geometric design.

The chitarra battente has a vaulted back of complex curvature, made of many ribs, and the incurved side walls are not of uniform width, being widest at the middle bouts. The soundboard, made of pine, bends back slightly beneath the bridge; the wire strings are plucked with a plectrum. Here, the instrument at the upper left shows a soundboard decorated with simple but charmingly stylized flowers, partly painted and partly inlaid with bone. The outstanding feature is the sunken sound hole, consisting of several rings of ornamentation, inlaid and painted, centered around a deep hole which is filled by a blue, yellow, and white paper flower. The chitarra battente below shows the beautiful design of the back, twenty strips of dark wood alternating with fine lines of white ivory inlay. The side walls, similarly, alternate strips of wood and ivory. The back of the neck is all of ivory, inlaid with a foliated pattern in black wax. The chitarra battente has been regarded as a descendent of the Spanish *vihuela da peñola*. However, the origin of the guitar and much of its early history are still in the dark. From the beginning of the seventeenth century, Italy was the classic land of the guitar. France, and of course Spain, took up the instrument with great enthusiasm.

New York, Metropolitan Museum of Art, 89.4.1037 (Crosby Brown Collection, 1889), 89.2.168, 89.2.169 (Drexel Collection). Background: 37.95.2, detail of printed cotton coverlet, Spain, late 18th century (Purchase, Rogers Fund, 1937).

50 51 *Violoncello*

sculptured by Domenico Galli, Parma, 1691

Violin

sculptured by Domenico Galli, Parma, 1687

Domenico Galli dedicated these outstanding showpieces to the Duke of Parma-Modena, Francesco II (1660–1694). There is a profusion of allegorical detail in the rich carving, and we are fortunate to find its interpretation in a description made by the historian, connoisseur, and collector L. F. Valdrighi at the end of the nineteenth century: "Di un'arpa, un violino e un violoncello che si conservano nell'odierno Museo Artistico Estense" (Modena, no date), p.12–15. He explains, among other things, the meaning of the carvings in two of the medallions on the back of this violoncello: he describes them as allusions to the dramatic religious and political events in England at that time. The sister of Duke Francesco II, Maria Beatrice, was the wife of King James II of England who, as a convert to Roman Catholicism, promoted pro-Catholic policies in England with the support of Spain and France. The lower medallion represents Maria Beatrice as Pallas Athena, together with a lion – evidently her son, James Francis Edward Stuart, Prince of Wales – subduing perfidy among the English. The central, smaller medallion shows Hercules killing the hydra, apparently another allusion to the Prince of Wales supposedly exterminating the unfaithful.

The back of the violin also has two medallions, the lower one being a representation of Orpheus. The deeply carved, rich leaf work covering the back of both instruments includes putti, satyrs, angels, and wild animals. The pegboxes are crowned by carved fruit and flowers; and a fantastic flying dragon emerges from them head down towards the finger board. The soundboards would of course never have tolerated carving as deep as that on the back; there, inlay is simulated by the painted black foliate scrolls. The violoncello is also decorated with a painted double eagle in the center. The heavy string holder, however, shows the same massive type of carving as the back.

Modena, Galleria Estense (Catalogue by Luisa Cervelli, "Mostra di Antichi Strumenti Musicali," Teatro Comunale, Comune di Modena, 1963–64, nos. 79 and 80).

VIOLON

Wann dorten Padua . mit seiner Gambe pranget
so leist ich bessre Dienst mit meinem Violon .
ich hab mit dieser Kunst unsterbliche Lob erlanget,
und heiß mit allem Recht ein wahrer Musen-Sohn:
weil meine Saiten selbst am Helicon erthönen .
wird einst Apollo noch die muntre Scheitel krönen,

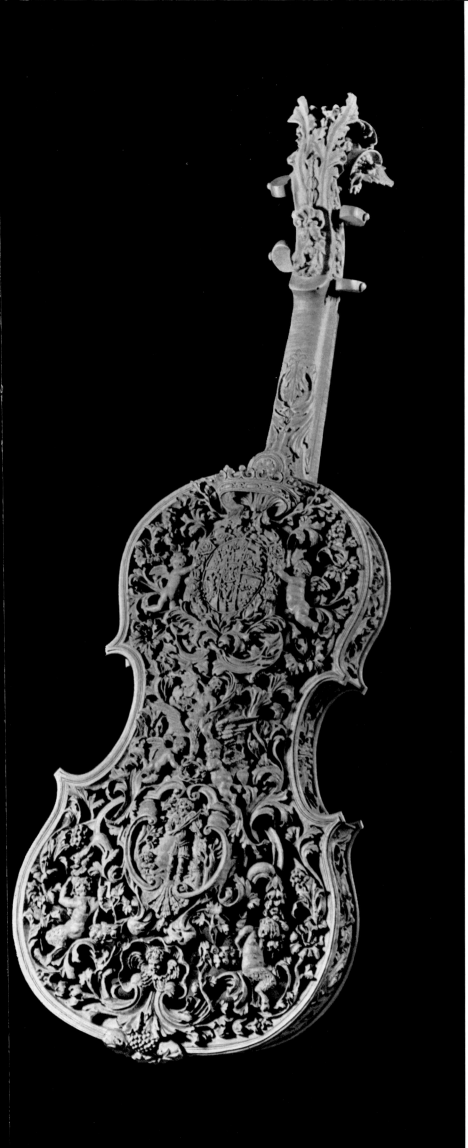

52 53 *Guitar and Violin of Marble*

Italian, 17th century (?)

These instruments, made of marble, are of course not functional, but are rather meant to be feasts for the eye. One could hardly imagine any material more remote than this heavy stone from the thin and feather-light wood of which guitars and violins are made. It must have been the intriguing harmonious shape of musical instruments that stimulated the imagination and artistic skill of marble cutters to try their hand at such a tour de force – a strong indication of the high esteem in which these patterns were held. How close the imitation of real instruments is one can judge by a comparison of these illustrations with that of a real guitar.

The high level of craftsmanship, especially the elegance of the foliate scrolls, seems to exclude a provincial origin; it seems rather probable that these pieces were executed in the grand-ducal workshops in Florence which contained the renowned *Officina delle Pietre Dure.*

Modena, Galleria Estense (Catalogue by Luisa Cervelli, Nos. 81 and 82).

54 *Pochette (Kit)*

German, 17th century (?) · With the false inscription: "Conradus Muller 1520." but dated 1690 in the Catalogue of the Musik Historiske Museum, Copenhagen, 1911

This pochette has the shape of a boat, which was frequent in the seventeenth century (pochette en bateau). The back of the neck has rich carving with figures, and the back of the pegbox a large grotesque face. The pegbox shows also an unusual feature: it is split in the middle and crowned on the front by two delicately carved heads.

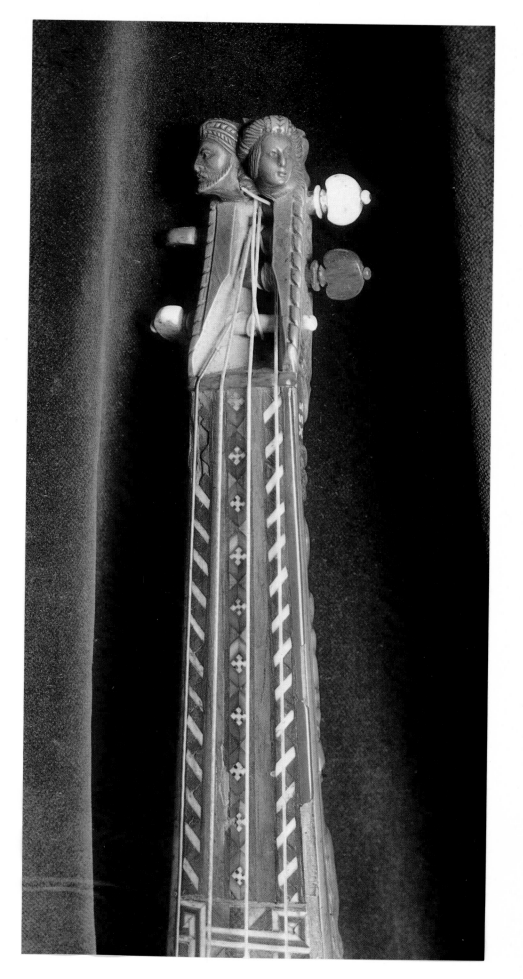

151

The author of the catalogue of the Musik Historiske Museum sees in the instrument "Albrecht Dürer's style"; but this is hardly tenable. Georg Kinsky, in his catalogue of the Wilhelm Heyer Collection in Cologne, 1912, Vol. II., p. 337, still refers to the date of 1520, regarding this instrument as probably the oldest dated pochette.

Copenhagen, Musik Historiske Museum (Catalogue by Hammerich, No. 55).

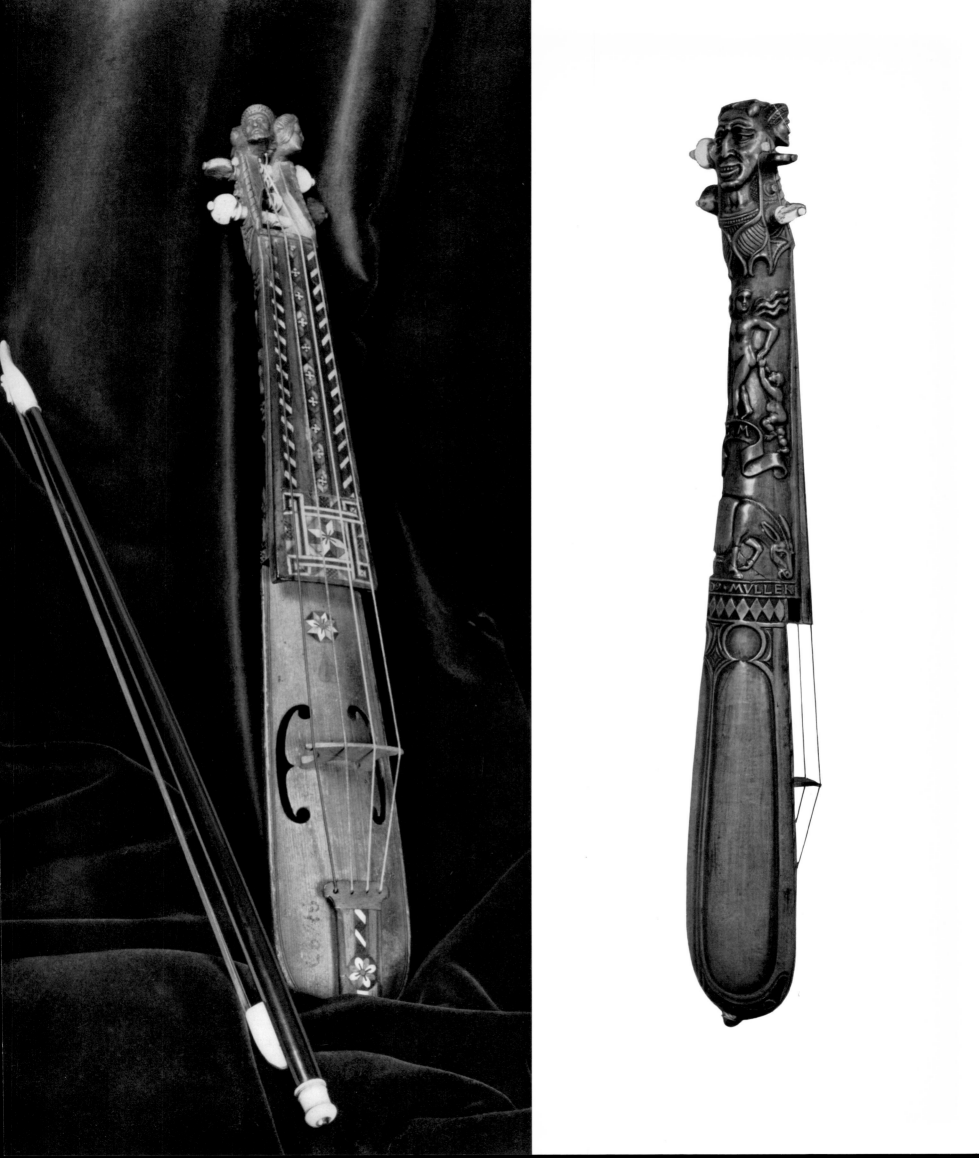

55 *Harpsichord*

Italian, mid-17th century

This harpsichord is of typical Italian make, with the instrument itself removable from an outer case. Functionally it differs from the prevailing type of clavicembalo of the time, because it has three sets of strings – one four-foot and two eight-foot. The common instruments, such as the harpsichord by Girolamo Zenti (Plate 36), had only two sets of eight-foot strings. Also its exquisite decoration surpasses the regular instruments. The body rests on three gilded columns; between the front columns is a mermaid holding one of them – the device of the Colonna family. The case is painted in sepia with beautiful floral scrolls in the free-flowing, majestic forms of the High Baroque. The keys are of ivory and ebony, the ebony ones having an inset strip of ivory. At each end of the keyboard there is a satyr of carved wood.

On the inside of the lid are two landscapes with figures in tempera. The front section shows, in an opulent setting of trees, Tobias and the Angel; the larger section shows an equally lush landscape with a duck hunter. The conventionalized foliage and the aerial perspective have the flavor of the work of Gaspard Dughet, Poussin's brother-in-law, who painted chiefly in Rome.

The instrument is in a miraculous state of preservation, as if it had been made only yesterday.
New York, Metropolitan Museum of Art. 45.41, Anonymous gift, 1945.

56 *Harpsichord*

made by Faby of Bologna, 1677,
for Count Hercule Pepoli, godson of Louis XIV.
Inscribed: "FABY BONONIENSIS OPUS ANNO DOMINI MDCLXXVII."

Faby, whose first name is not known to us, was a Bolognese harpsichord maker who settled in Paris, where two of his magnificent, lavishly decorated instruments are still preserved in the Conservatoire de Musique. The construction and ornamentation of both of these instruments is characteristically Italian.

The harpsichord shown here has a fine rose of geometrical design in the soundboard. The inside of the side walls, the jackrail, and the frontboard are inlaid with ivory, ebony, and mother-of-pearl. Small ivory buttons decorate all the edges. The keys – four octaves and two notes, acting on two sets of eight-foot strings – are also lavishly ornamented: the black keys are centered with ivory strips, and the back of the white keys are inlaid, as are their arcaded front slabs. The front board carries in the center the coat of arms of Count Hercule Pepoli, godson of Louis XIV, and this coat of arms is connected by a ribbon to *mascheroni* and to two oblong cartouches showing landscapes, which flank the center. Flanking the entire frontboard are designs showing swans with jingle bells around their necks.

There is an outer case, as was usual in Italian harpsichords, and the inside of the lid is painted to represent a mountain landscape with a lake, two castles, and several strolling couples. The side walls of the case simulate marble inlay, with strapwork of white bands and brown filling on a dark blue background.

Clapisson Collection, Musée instrumental du Conservatoire Nationale de Musique, Paris,
No. E. 224 C 328.

Italian, mid-17th century

This monumental, gilded harpsichord is undoubtedly one of the most striking pieces of Baroque furniture in existence. The wing-shaped body of the instrument is supported by three fishtailed Tritons, gliding on softly swelling waves. Between them rise two sea nymphs, and riding behind is a putto, perched high on a sea shell and driving two dolphins. All these fishy folk move through the water with bold and cheerful gestures. The water itself, silvery green and shimmering, is enclosed by a massive ledge that repeats on a larger scale the outline of the harpsichord proper. And this whole oceanic phantasmagoria rests on lions' feet. The right side of the harpsichord is decorated with an elaborate gilded frieze representing the triumph of Galatea. Sitting in a wheeled shell car drawn by fishtailed horses, Galatea travels over the waves; trumpeting Tritons herald her approach and follow her carriage. Putti, some of them winged, ride sea horses, and everywhere one can see a gay medley of fins, spiraling tails, and agitated horses. Even the clouds in the background participate in the interplay of moving curves. On the extreme left, next to a span of three wildly excited horses, yet quite removed from all the watery commotion, sits the only tranquil figure in the frieze, an idyllic youthful musician on a rock. In contrast to the other creatures, who blow on trumpets, he plays a stringed instrument, the noble lute.

The harpsichord in its basin is flanked by two life-sized figures, each sitting on a rock. Both, like the harpsichord, are made of gilded wood. The one on the left represents Polyphemus; the right, Galatea. Polyphemus plays a bagpipe. Galatea's instrument is missing, but to judge from the position of her arms and fingers, she probably had a lute. Here Polyphemus is not the ferocious man-eating and rock-throwing giant of the *Odyssey*, who devoured Ulysses' companions and crushed Galatea's lover with a stone, but the longing, unhappy shepherd, saddened and dandified by his unrequited love for the nymph, as we find him in Alexandrian poetry and particularly in Ovid's *Metamorphoses* (Book XIII).

Two lucky findings contribute to the history of this fantastic instrument.[9] After World War II, in the basement storerooms of the Palazzo Venezia in Rome, among heaps of debris salvaged from bomb sites, a box turned up filled with small reddish clay fragments. When these were assembled, they appeared to form the small clay model of this harpsichord and its flanking figures, evidently made either for the patron who ordered the instrument or as a working guide for the execution of the instrument by the wood carvers. Some more light was thrown on our instrument by an amusing book published in Rome in 1676, the *Galleria Armonica* by Michele Todini, who had been a musician in the service of the Pope and later founded a museum of musical instruments which he described in his book. In the third chapter, he describes "*la macchina di Polifemo e Galatea*," which is nothing else than our instrument. Apparently at that time it was equipped with a magic device: the keyboard of the harpsichord was connected by hidden wires to a set of pipes hidden in the mountain of Polyphemus, which supplied the sound of his bagpipe or, to quote the book, showed Polyphemus "in the act of playing a sordellina to please Galatea." The instrument was known to have once been in the possession of the Viscount Sartiges, who was the French ambassador to the Holy See in the 1860's. It entered the Metropolitan Museum of Art in 1889 as part of the Crosby Brown Collection.

New York, Metropolitan Museum of Art, 89.4.2929 (Crosby Brown Collection, 1889).

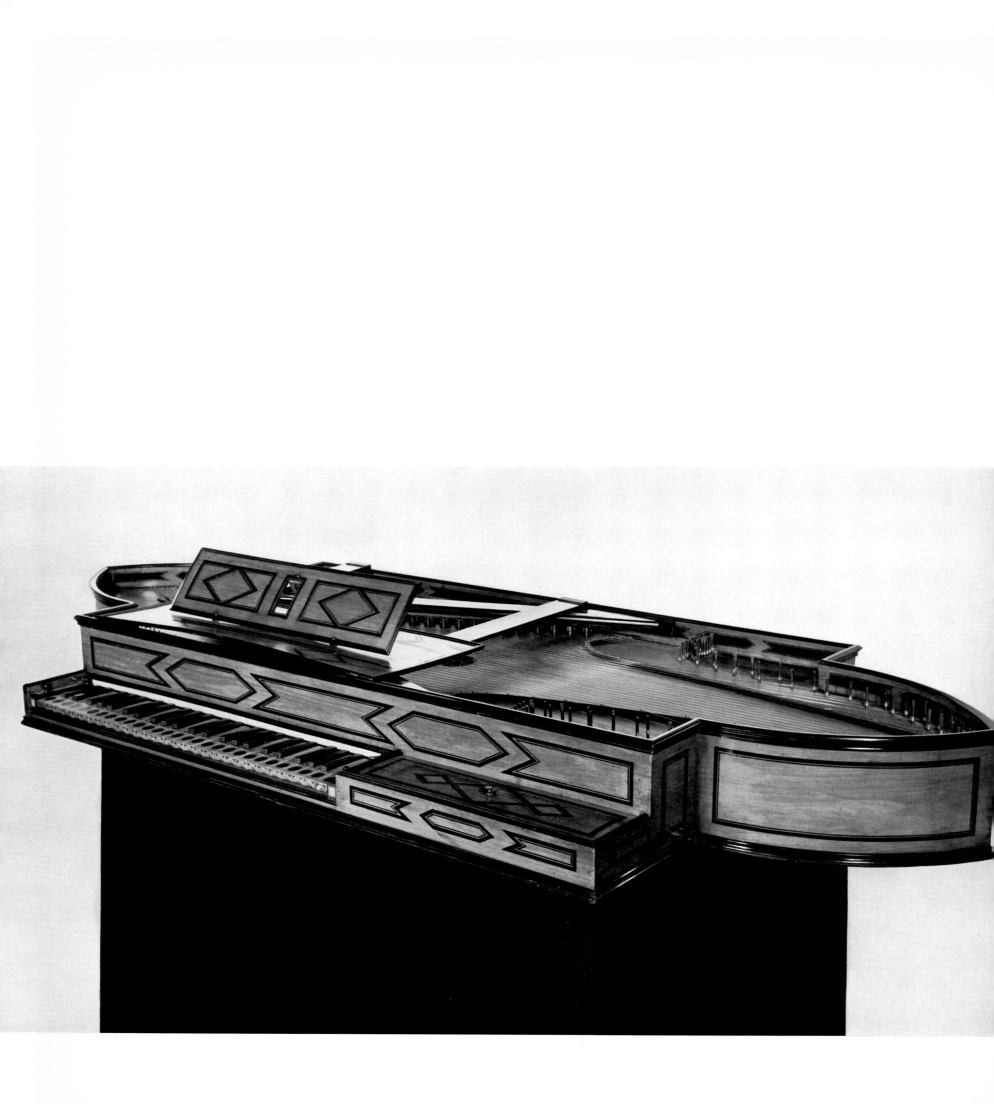

58 *Spinet*

*by Bartolommeo Cristofori, Florence, 1693 · Inscribed inside the string box to the right of the keyboard, "Bartholomaeus Christophori Patavinus/Faciebat Florentiae/*MDCXCIII*"*

Bartolommeo Cristofori was the celebrated inventor of the pianoforte – or, as he called it, *"gravicembalo col piano e forte"* – the keyboard instrument which enabled the player to produce crescendos and decrescendos, effects not possible on the harpsichords and organs of his time Christofori was originally a harpsichord maker in Padua, his birthplace; between 1687 and 1690 he was called as official *cembalaro* to the Medici court at Florence where, apart from his experiments with the pianoforte, he continued building harpsichords.

Among those instruments was this spinet, which is of a construction so different from traditional spinets that one is at once reminded of the searching spirit and imagination of this master craftsman. The oblong soundboard terminates in pointed arches, and the arrangement of the strings is highly unusual: there are two oblique bridges meeting at a sharp angle and, correspondingly, two separate rows of jacks with their jack rails (of which only one is visible here, at the rear of the soundboard). This unique system results in an even distribution of the pressure of the strings throughout the case

Another unusual feature is the exquisite decoration: well-spaced geometrical inlays of ebony all over the side walls, frontboard, string box, and music stand. The soundboard has an elegant rose (partly visible here) carved out of cypress wood, with the Florentine emblem formed by flowers. This rose must have been especially appreciated and valued by both the builder of the instrument and its receiver, for in the bill for the instrument, preserved in the Florentine state archives, it is especially mentioned and prized. The bill is made out to Ferdinand dei Medici, who was the eldest son of the Grand Duke Cosimo III; it is this same prince who had met Cristofori in Padua and arranged for him to be employed at the court in Florence.

Leipzig, Karl-Marx-Universität. (No. 53 in the Catalogue by Georg Kinsky of the Musikhistorisches Museum of Wilhelm Heyer in Cologne, 1910.)

POSAUNE

Ich suche fast den Ruhm an allen Ort und Enden,
so wohl den Alterthum als auch der Würkung nach,
man sehe was ich kan in beeden Testamenten,
ich warff die Mauren ein als man mich recht besprach,
kein Opffer oder Fest wird recht ohn mich vollführet
und heunt zu Tag bin ich was grosse Chör bezieret.

59 *Quartbass-Trombone*

Inscribed: "M. Joh. Leonhr Ehe i Nurnb(erg) 1732."

This Quartbass-trombone, at once machine and work of art, is a showpiece of outstanding beauty. The brass tube of considerable length – no less than 435 cm – is bent four times into five close parallel pieces of tubing held together by three crossbars and a broad band.

The instrument has two slides to enable the player to achieve any pitch desired. The slides are manipulated by long brass sticks with elaborately carved wooden handles. By the eight-

162

eenth century trombone slides were by no means a novelty; slides of this kind can be clearly recognized in Italian pictures as early as the beginning of the sixteenth century.

The bell of our instrument opens up into a broad rim richly decorated with a male face, possibly a portrait, and five winged heads of angels.

Johann Leonhard Ehe came from a reputed Nuremberg family of makers of brass instruments; illustrated in Plate 41 is a Quintbass-trombone made in the year 1612 by Johann Isaak Ehe.

Vienna, Kunsthistorisches Museum; property of the Gesellschaft der Musikfreunde No. 202 (inventory by E. Mandyczewski). Background: dark-blue damask silk from the canopy of an eighteenth-century bed from Schlosshof, Österreichisches Museum für Angewandte Kunst, Vienna-T 9054.

60 *Jagdhorn (hunting horn)*

by Michael Leichamschneider, Vienna, 1713
Inscribed on bell rim: "M. Leichamschneider 1713"

Michael Leichamschneider was a well-known Viennese maker of trumpets and horns. The instrument illustrated here is of silver with gilded decorations. The bell rim shows, in relief, four riders on horseback and the maker's name.

Related in shape and tone to the post horn and early Waldhorn, this instrument is characterized by the conoidal shape of the tube, the deep throat of its mouthpiece, and the wide rim of its bell.

Kunsthistorisches Museum, Vienna (Inventory No. 598).

61 *Hunting Horn*

France, c. 1700

Hunting horns in the Middle Ages were often made of ox or cow horns; and when other materials were used, the instruments were still made to follow the natural horn shape. From a somewhat later period, this short, slightly curved horn is made of ivory in the shape of a fish-like monster, with carved gills, scales, and fins. The head, however, rather resembles that of a crocodile, holding in its teeth the cup-shaped mouthpiece. An ivory ring attached to the top of the horn provides a place for a cord to be strung, by which the hunter could carry the instrument.

This horn is a type of signal instrument used by shepherds, watchmen, soldiers, and hunters, and is called, in old German, *Hifthorn* (not from *Hüfte*, meaning "hip," but from *hift* or *hief*, which denoted the sound of hunting horns).

New York, Metropolitan Museum of Art, 89.4.1485 (Crosby Brown Collection, 1889).

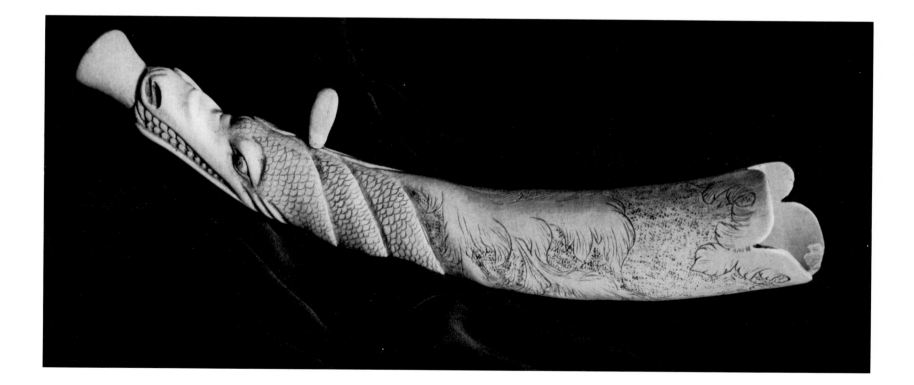

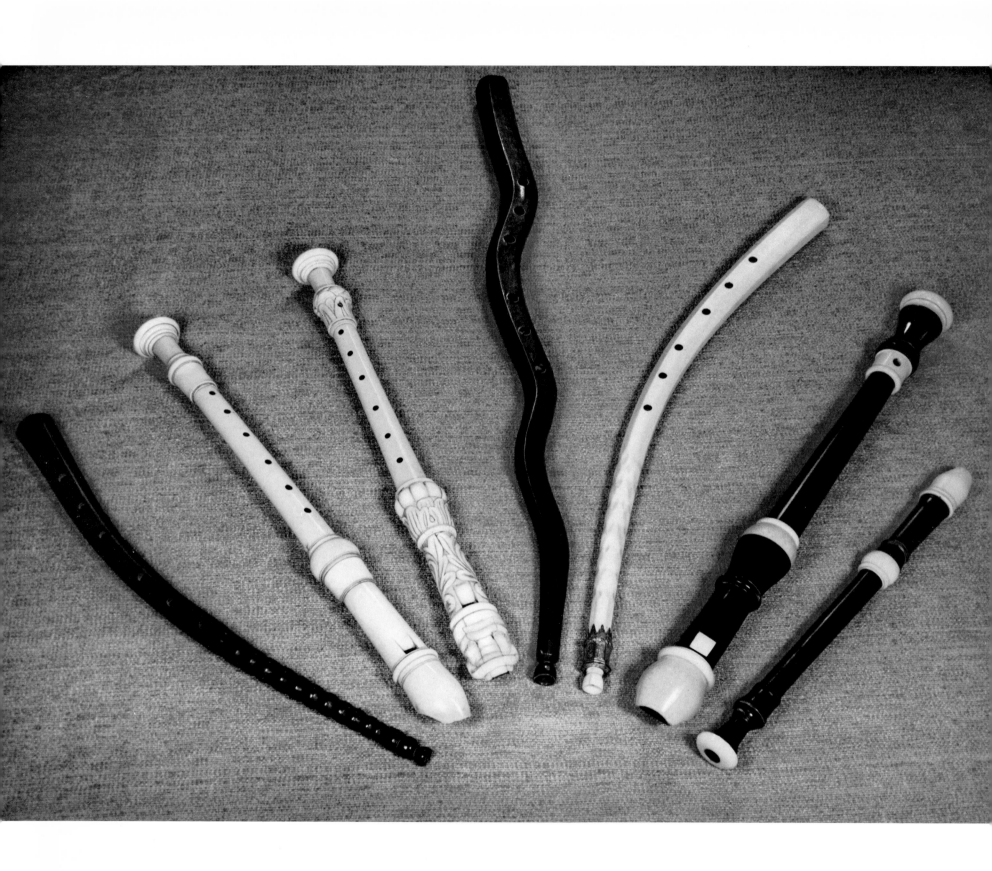

From left to right:

62 *(1)* **Cornetto à Bouquin (Cornetto Curvo)**
treble size, France, early 17th century

(2) **Recorder (Blockflöte) in F**
Germany, 17th century

(3) **Recorder (Flûte Douce) in F**
France, 17th century

(4) **Cornet à Bouquin (Cornetto Torto)**
tenor in B flat, Italy, early 17th century

(5) **Zink (Cornetto Curvo)**
treble size, Germany, 17th or late 16th century

(6) **Recorder (Blockflöte)**
alto in F, Germany(?), 18th century

(7) **Recorder (Blockflöte)**
treble in B flat, Germany, 18th century
*Inscribed: "*T. BOEKHOUT*" with a crown and a lion above and below the name*

This group of seventeenth and eighteenth-century wind instruments—cornetti and record-ers—reveals a great variety of shapes and decoration. Numbers 1, 4, and 5 (numbering from left to right) are different versions of the cornetto, the only wind instrument that combines a cup-shaped mouthpiece (comparable to that of a trumpet) with a tube equipped with side holes. The cornetto made great demands on the player's lip technique and had a brilliant but mellow rather than piercing tone. Mersenne compared it to a ray of sunshine cutting through the clouds. It was widely used in the seventeenth and eighteenth centuries in the orchestra of Monteverdi and the Gabrielis, and up to the time of Bach, Handel, and even Gluck.

There were several forms of straight cornetti which could be turned and bored on a lathe. The curved variants (cornetto curvo and cornetto torto) were not so easy to make: they were formed of two long slabs of wood which were hollowed out to achieve the appropriate conoidal bore and then glued together and covered, usually, with black leather (Nos. 1 and 4). The most difficult work of drilling was involved in making a curved ivory cornetto such as our No. 5. This outstanding specimen also shows the characteristic diamond pattern on the upper part of the tube, and an elegant gilded mounting near the upper end. The ivory mouthcup is the original one made for the instrument.

Of the four recorders shown here (Nos. 2, 3, 6, and 7), the first two are made of ivory, the second one being exquisitely carved with a foliage design and having its mouthpiece shaped in the form of a fishlike monster. The other two recorders have typical eighteenth-century profiles, with broad rings at the joints. The alto recorder (No. 6) is made of ebony in three parts; the treble recorder is of stained wood in two parts; in both instruments the rings and mouthpieces are made of ivory.

New York, Metropolitan Museum of Art. 89.4.1670, 89.4.908, 89.4.909, 89.4.2142, 89.4.912 (Crosby Brown Collection, 1889); 52.96.1 (Purchase, 1952); 53.56.15 (Gift of the University Museum, University of Pennsylvania, 1953).

63 *Transverse Flute in B*

Paris, ca. 1700 · Stamped: "Hotteterre," with the anchor trademark

Oboe

Paris, ca. 1692 · Marked: "Dupuis"

This flute, made of reddish boxwood with ivory mounts, is made in four parts: head cap, head with the embouchure and a broad ivory ring, body with finger holes, and a short foot joint with brass key.

The oboe, likewise of boxwood with strongly projecting ivory mounts, is made in three parts: two body joints, each with three finger holes, and a bell. The brass keys are protected by a broad, perforated ivory ring. The bore, as in all oboes, is conical.

These instruments are exact contemporaries and show, despite their different functional shapes, the same taste in profiling and color combinations. The second half of the seventeenth century and the eighteenth century were the golden age of the *traversière* and the oboe; one needs only to recall the role given to them in the orchestra by J. S. Bach and by Mozart—especially in combination with the human voice; and the various instructions written for them, from Jacques Hotteterre's *Principes de la flute traversiere* (Paris, 1707) to Johann Joachim Quantz's *Versuch einer Anweisung, die Flöte traversiere zu spielen* (Berlin, 1752), and the *New and Compleat Instructions for the Oboe or Hoboy* by T, Cahusac (London, ca. 1790).

Hotteterre was the name of a celebrated family of French musicians in the seventeenth and eighteenth centuries, comprising several generations of performing musicians, instrument makers, composers, and teachers. The trademark of the anchor has been associated with Jean Hotteterre (Haulteterre); but since he may have left it to his heirs, it is not possible to attribute the flute to him with absolute certainty.

The player of the *flute traversière* in the background is Ferdinand Semberger, portrayed by his friend Jan Kupetzky in 1710. Kupetzky was a celebrated painter of historical subjects and genre, born in 1667 in Pressburg (at that time in Hungary). He traveled widely in Italy, and found important patrons at the Imperial court in Vienna. Later, for religious reasons, he was forced to flee to Nuremberg, where he died in 1740.

Berlin, Staatliche Musikinstrumentensammlung (Catalogue by Curt Sachs, No. 2670—flute; 2933—oboe).

64 *Cittern*

Italian, 1700

This instrument is of the finest workmanship with its six double strings attached to three rows of four pegs each, and eighteen frets. The belly has a simple, circular, open sound hole with double purflings, while the neck has a large hook at the back and ends in a delicately carved female head. This neck section is decorated by exquisite carving showing figures, *mascheroni*, and floral designs. The back of the body is composed of six slightly concave strips of reddish maple separated by purflings. Most characteristic of citterns of that time, besides the hook mentioned, are the little carved figure on the lower left side of the finger board and the two little scroll-shaped projections at the meeting point of body and neck; the latter are rudiments of the large ears which are found in Italian Quattrocento citterns and which, in their turn, were atrophic remnants of the arms of the ancient kithara.

This cittern, dated 1700 by the Conservatoire, has occasionally been attributed to Antonio Stradivari, although such authorities as the Hill family, while having admiration for its workmanship, refute this claim in their book on this master (*Antonio Stradivari*, by W. Henry Hill, Arthur F. Hill, and Alfred E. Hill).

Paris, Musée Instrumental du Conservatoire National de Musique, E 1271, C 1053.

65 **Cittern (detail)**

D. P. Jovanni Salvatori, Italy (undated, 17th century?)

In this head of a cittern, functional elements, such as the crownshaped pegs, are united with the carved female head and the sharp hook to form an aesthetic unit of bizarre appeal. To a child's or poet's eye, it might almost appear that the noble lady bends forward to count her pawns.

Paris, Musée Instrumental du Conservatoire National de Musique, E 543, C 250 (Anc. Coll.: Dr. Fau).

Right plate below: Back of Cittern 64 (see page 172/173)

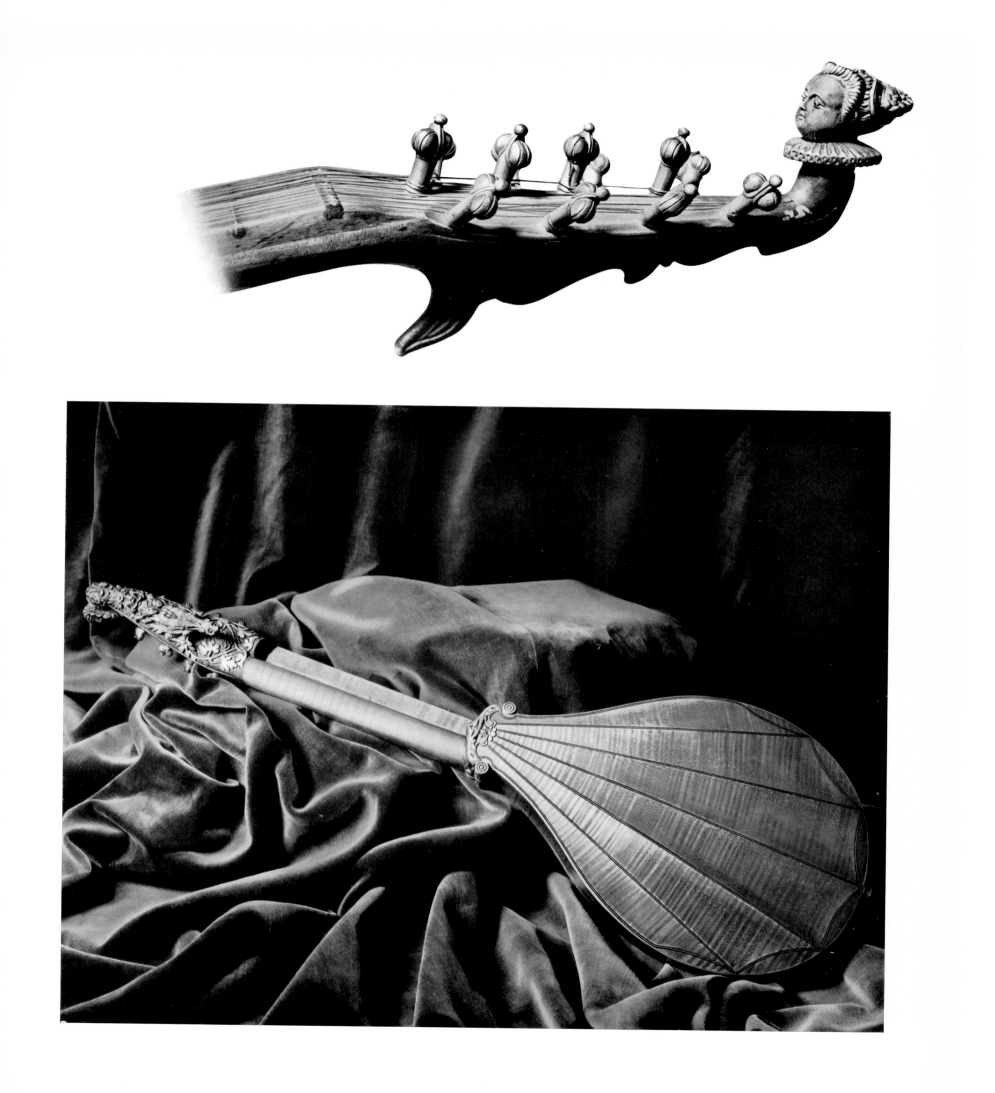

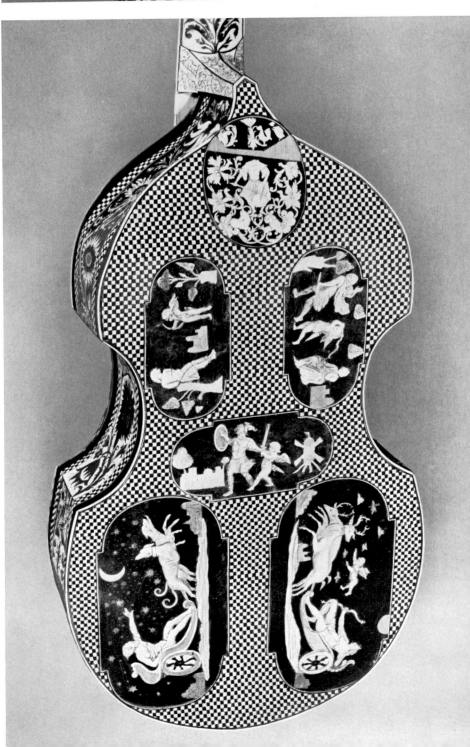

66 *Viola da Gamba*

Inscribed: "Joachim Tielcke in Hamburg/An. 1691"

This and the following Plates 67 and 68 show different instruments by Joachim Tielcke. A comparison reveals how an original instrument maker with a subtle imagination applied different decorative schemes to different instruments, and also how the style of his decorative patterns changed within a few years.

Tielcke was the most celebrated lute maker of his time. About his early life and his teachers nothing is known. Possibly he spent some time as an apprentice in Italy; certain features in his instruments lead to this assumption. In 1669 he became a citizen of Hamburg. There he died in 1719, famous in Germany and many other lands for his lutes, viols, and other instruments. This plate shows one of his glamorous instruments, executed in his fiftieth year when he was at the peak of his career. No wonder that his instruments were sought after – as we learn from contemporary reports – by many great performers from near and far, and that he received "for one single lute 100 Mark or 50 Gulden," a record price at the time.

With the exception of its soundboard, the whole instrument is covered with an inlay of ivory, ebony, tortoise shell, silver, and mother-of-pearl. The decorative pattern on the side walls, the finger board, and the string holder appear in black on white ground. The pegbox, crowned by a head of Minerva, is carved of ivory. A curious decorative scheme is applied to the back: into a checkerboard pattern of small white and black squares several medallions are inserted; the two largest ones represent Diana and Saturn, three smaller ones show episodes with Cupid, and an oval one near the shoulder presents a player of a viola da gamba surrounded by foliate scrolls. All the figures here, in contrast to the decorative scheme on the other parts of the instrument, appear white against black. The shape of the medallions form a sort of awkward contrast to the waisted contour of the instrument.

Munich, Bayerisches Nationalmuseum, No. 39.

67 *Hamburger Cithrinchen (Bell Cittern)*

Hamburg, about 1700 · Inscribed on the side of the neck: "Joachim Tielcke in Ham. 1539"
(The date is in another hand.)

This charming variety of the cittern (see Plate 8) was fashionable in Germany towards the end of the seventeenth century. It had the contour of a bell, five double strings, and a slightly arched back.

The present specimen is virtually covered by marquetry in tortoise shell and ivory, and studded with little gems of colored glass or paste. In design the marquetry consists of floral patterns and, on the back, two triumphs: that of Galatea on her car drawn by dolphins, and that of Diana on a vehicle drawn by stags. The long pegbox has a wooden finial in the shape of a woman's head, studded with pieces of ivory to simulate strings of pearls. Only three of the ten pegs are original; the frets are of silver. The date, incised on the neck, is in a different hand from the signature and without doubt is spurious. – In design and decorative scheme this instrument is characteristic of Tielcke's workshop, though the two "triumphs" lack his usual elegance.

London, Victoria and Albert Museum, 1122–1869.

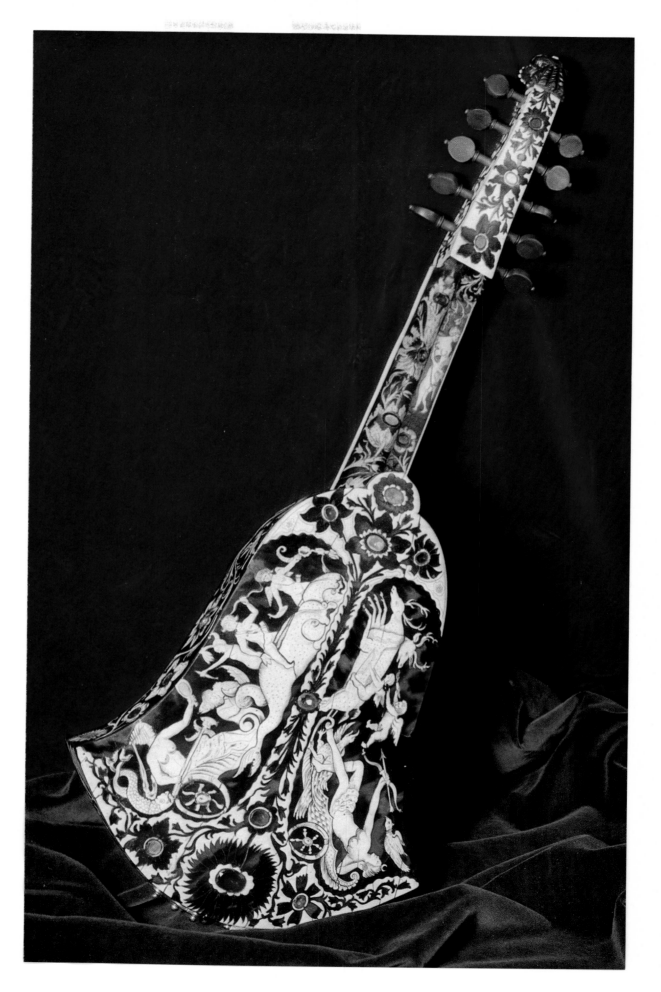

179

68 *Guitar*

by Joachim Tielcke · Inscribed on the neck: "Tielcke." Germany, 17th Century

The decoration of this instrument is perhaps the most harmonious among all the many show-pieces created by Tielcke. It is inlaid with ivory, ebony, tortoise shell, silver, and mother-of-pearl. The slightly arched back is composed of three broad ivory sections separated by thin black strips while the marquetry shows arabesques of foliate scrolls with five inserted medallions in tortoise shell representing various episodes with Cupid. The side walls have a series of large and small medallions showing scenes with Orpheus, Amorini, and other subjects. On both sides the neck has motifs with vines and flowers.

The great subtlety of Tielcke's decorative genius is revealed in the distribution of black and white patterns in the marquetry. On its front the neck shows large white flowers against black background, and on the back the reverse is true; the back of the body has dark figures in tortoise shell against white background. The medallions on the side walls have white figures against black. This type of decoration is perhaps the most sophisticated among the several devised by the almost inexhaustible imagination of this master craftsman.

New Haven, Yale University, Collection of Musical Instruments.

180

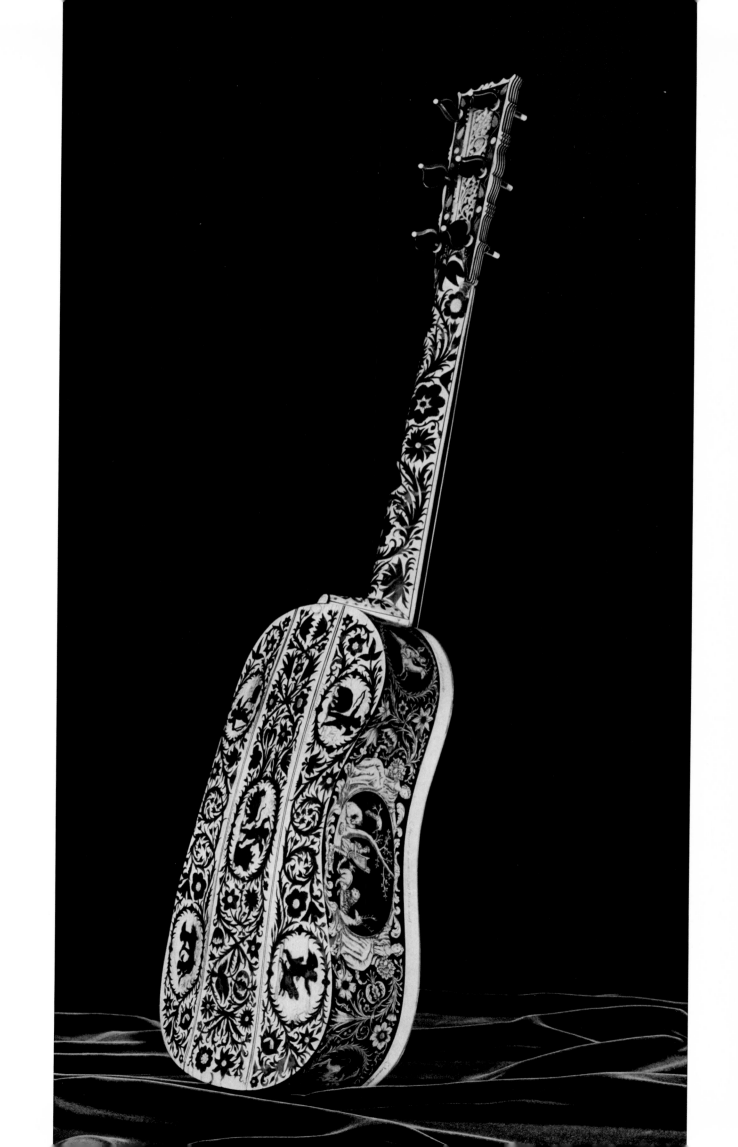

69 *Viola d'Amore*

Inscribed "CASPAR STADLER TRABANT IN MÜNCHEN 1714 A.D."

This viola d'amore is in many ways similar to the one illustrated in Plate 49; but it has a more shallow body and its decoration is of a totally different conception. It is an outstanding example of German eighteenth-century design. The foliate scrolls in the viola d'amore by Klotz are in black on a white background; in the present instrument they appear white against black; here however, they are not in a homogeneous pattern but in a layout that cleverly exploits the tripartite shape of the instrument's body. The upper section is triangular and accommodates two small figures with wind instruments; the middle section, corresponding to the waist, has its independent scheme of grotesques and also includes two musicians, one with a harp, the other with a shawm or trumpet. The lowest compartment has, in addition to grotesques, a more realistic depiction of musicians: a small table with a dancing dog is flanked by two sitting ladies; the one at the left tunes a cittern, a lute leaning behind her; the one at the right bows a viola da gamba. These figures are laid on in silver and brass.

Caspar Stadler, born probably in Füssen, is known chiefly for his violins characterized by highly arched bellies and dark varnish.

Nuremberg, Germanisches Nationalmuseum, No. M I 208.

70 *Two Violins*

The "Antonius" (at the left), signed
"Antonius Stradivarius Cremonensis/Faciebat
Anno 1721" (date somewhat blurred)

The "Francesca", signed
"Antonius Stradivarius Cremonensis/
Faciebat Anno 1694"

Books written about the violin – its history, its construction, and the beauty of its shape, proportions, and tone – would fill many shelves. The origin and early history of the violin are still not completely known. The violin was no "invention" but the result of a long evolution and fusion of a number of elements which occurred separately, in earlier stringed instruments: for instance, in the shallow German and Italian fiddles of the fifteenth century, in the family of the *viola da gamba*, and of the *lira da braccio*. Only after the middle of the sixteenth century, at the time of the great dynasties of violin makers, did something like a standard form crystallize, though still with minor variations in proportions, arching, tone color, etc.

When the violin first tried to compete with the silver-voiced viol, it was maligned as an ignoble, shrieking, vulgar instrument; and one could hardly have foreseen then that it would become and remain the queen of the orchestra and one of the most important protagonists in chamber music. Only gradually was its wide range of expression, from sweet cantabile to greatest dramatic force, realized and exploited. One of the important factors which helped its victory was a great new achievement of the Baroque, the opera, where a loud and flexible stringed instrument was needed. Two facts are remarkable above all: first, that out of a maze of tentative forms, the form of the violin finally crystallized; and second, that as soon as it had been accepted, it remained basically the same in shape up to our day, although of course modern playing techniques required minor changes in stringing methods and in the length and angle of the finger board.

A magic aura surrounds the violins of the celebrated masters of the seventeenth and eighteenth centuries. Antonio Stradivari, who was born in 1644, probably in Cremona, and died there in 1737, is probably the most famous of all. His individual patterns and their change throughout his long life are the subject of numerous monographs. This plate illustrates two of his violins. At the left is the so-called "Antonius" (1721 – blurred), which shows its beautiful back made of maple, in two pieces, sparingly flamed and cut on the quarter grain. At the right is the "Francesca" (1694), a specimen of the long pattern which was introduced about 1690 and definitely discarded about 1700. We see here its evenly and closely grained pine belly, with the finely cut F-shape sound holes.

One of the most interesting elements of the violin is its scroll. The intriguing shape of the spiral is frequent in nature and in art. In nature, it occurs in water whirls, in sea shells, snails, and animal horns, and in the cores of certain blossoms. Man-made spirals are found in early periods of art – in Mycenean metalwork and pottery in the Dipylon style, in the volutes of Ionic capitals, and later in countless versions in the visual idiom of the Baroque, to mention only a few examples. How did it come to assume its important role as violin head in the six-

Antonins Stradiuarius Cremonensis
Faciebat Anno 1694

But in spite of their small size, some pochettes (or "poches") must have been sweet and sonorous enough in tone to be used for performance in ensembles. A mid-seventeenth-century verse says:

> "*Trois masques qui se présentèrent*
> *Ayant requis d'entrer, entrèrent.*
> *Et tirant soudain de leur poche*
> *Chacun une petite poche,*
> *Sans être longs à l'accorder*
> *Et sans peu ni point préluder*
> *Jouèrent une sarabande."*

New York, Metropolitan Museum of Art, 89.4.969, 89.4.967 (Crosby Brown Collection, 1889); 58.158 (purchase, Rogers Fund, 1956); 64.72 (gift of Aaron Schoenbaum, 1964). Background: 35.60, blue silk waistcoat, French, 18th century, (gift of Norman Rockwell, 1935).

72 *Viola d'amore Kit (Pochette)*

Germany, ca. 1700

Occasionally, pochettes were constructed in the shape and with the sympathetic strings of the *Viola d'amore*. The instrument pictured here has six gut strings and six sympathetic strings of wire, the latter passing through tiny holes in the bridge and running under the finger board. Its long body has very narrow side walls which are, in fact, only the thickness of the belly and back of the instrument, which meet there. However, the belly and back are so strongly arched that the sound box is of considerable height at the bridge. The belly has purflings and the characteristic long and flaming sound holes of the viola d'amore.

The neck and head of the instrument are of exquisite beauty, the head carved to represent a blindfolded Cupid, whose tiny wings curve down to join the pegbox. The upper part of the pegbox, where the sympathetic strings are held, is covered by a gracefully carved leafy scroll. This carved scrollwork covers only the back (not visible here) of the lower part of the pegbox, since the strings attached there must be free to run over the finger board.

New York, Metropolitan Museum of Art. 89.4.2426 (Crosby Brown Collection, 1889).

73 *Hurdy-Gurdy*

France, 17th century

The hurdy-gurdy (vielle à roue, Drehleier, ghironda) is a sort of mechanized fiddle whose strings are set into vibration by the rim of a wooden wheel revolving in the middle of the sound box and turned by a crank at its tail end. The smooth edge of the wheel, which is coated with resin, serves as an endless bow. There are melody strings ("*chanterelles*") running along the middle of the sound box; and open ones, the drones ("*bourdons*"), running on either side. The melody strings are stopped by a primitive key mechanism, a set of stopping rods —naturals and sharps— equipped with little projections that press inward against the strings when the rods are pushed. Thus a full scale can be produced. When released, the rods fall back of their own weight. The two melody strings are tuned in unison, the drones in octaves.

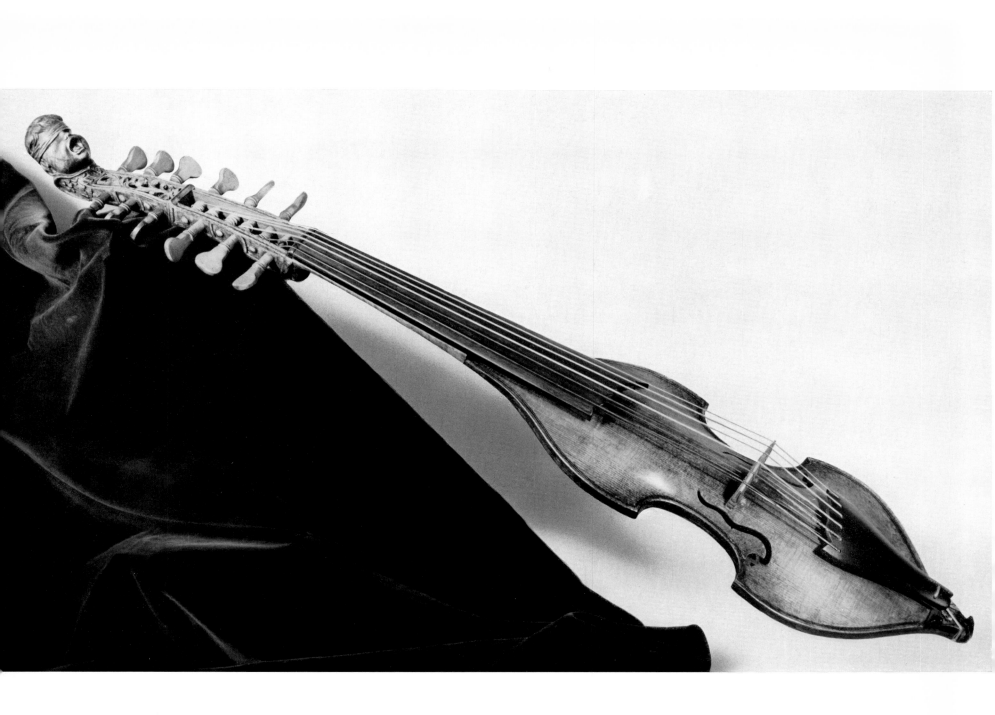

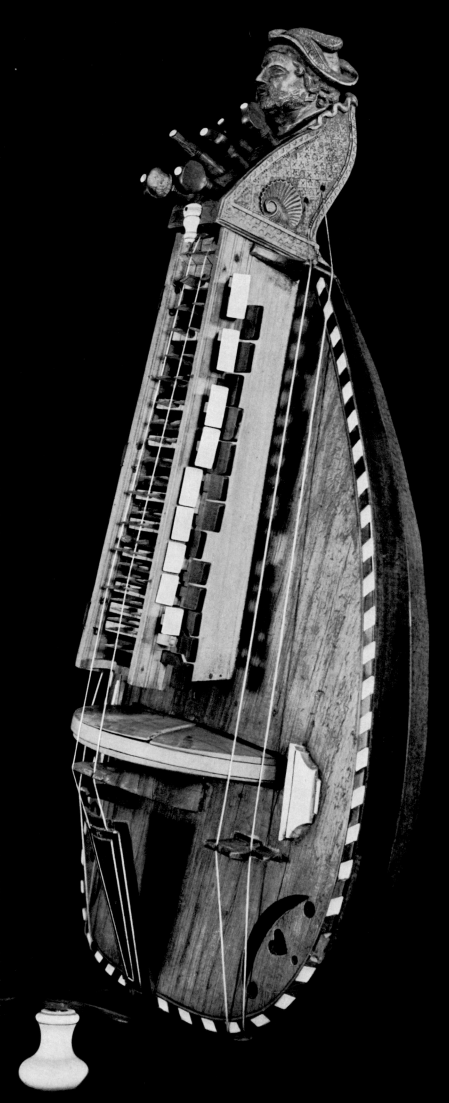

The hurdy-gurdy is of venerable age; it appeared first in the tenth century under the name "organistrum"—an ungainly, large instrument that needed two men to operate it: one turned the crank, the other used both hands for manipulating the slow and awkward stopping mechanism. Such, at least, were the instruments which we find in representations of the Elders of the Apocalypse in the sculptures of the cathedrals of Moissac, Santiago de Compostela, and other Romanesque churches.

It is the drone principle, shared also by the bagpipe—i.e., the accompaniment of a melody by an invariable bass—that gives the hurdy-gurdy and its music their special character.

Since the Middle Ages the hurdy-gurdy repeatedly changed social status. We find it in the hands of beggars and jugglers, played by monsters in the drolleries inhabiting the margins of fourteenth and fifteenth century illuminations and Books of Hours, and later in the hands of angels in the countless celestial concerts depicted in Renaissance art. Still later, under the impact of the French pastoral fashion introduced by Giovanni Battista Guarini's drama *Il Pastor Fido*, it became—largely because of its bagpipe-like drone—a shepherd instrument, or rather pseudo-shepherd instrument, played by perfumed shepherds and shepherdesses in the *Fêtes Champêtres* of the Trianon and Fontainebleau.

The hurdy-gurdy has had various shapes, the most important being that of a guitar and that of a lute. (Actually the bodies of many lutes survived because they were converted into hurdy-gurdies.) The present illustration shows a hurdy-gurdy with the bulging back of a lute. The soundboard has two C-shaped sound holes near the tail end, and its edge is inlaid with ebony and ivory. The touch pieces for the stopping rods are likewise of ebony and ivory. Its most sumptuously decorated part is the pegbox; it terminates in a bearded head of a pilgrim with the symbolical conch shell on his head; larger conch shells are carved also into the sides of the pegbox.

New York, Metropolitan Museum of Art, 89.4.1059 (Crosby Brown Collection, 1889).

74 *Hurdy-Gurdy Organ (Orgel-Leier, Vielle Organisée)*

France, 18th century

This instrument combines two realms of sound: strings and pipes. It is, in other words, a hurdy-gurdy with pipes—in fact a little organ—added. Unlike the lute-shaped hurdy-gurdy (see Plate 13), this instrument has a guitar-shaped body with the usual six strings (two melody strings in the center to be stopped by twenty-four stopping rods, and two pairs of drone strings) and a friction wheel, hidden from view by its semicircular cover. When these keys were pushed by the player, the rods not only stopped the melody strings but also opened valves leading air from a wind chest to the wooden pipes that are arranged in two triangular sets, one on top of another, resembling two sets of Panpipes. At the left is the crank that turns the wheel; at the right the pegbox terminates in the customary carved head. The deep body of the instrument contains the bellows which probably were connected to a rope and worked by

LEYRERIN.

Heÿ luſtig junge Purſch, thut euch nur munder halten
ſeird fröhlich weil ihr köñt, ſo lang es euch behagt:
im Feld wird manchem bald das freudge Hertz erkalten,
wañ ſtatt des Leÿren-thon, der Stücke-Donner kracht
da gilt ein andrer tantz; man wird mich gar nicht achten
Ein tapfferer Soldat, der muß nach Sieg nur trachten.

the player's feet. The soundboard and the boxes containing the pipes are of mahogany, the side walls of walnut.

This combination of wind and string sound in one single instrument is one of the several fulfilments of an age-old musician's dream; another was the clavi-organum, the combination of a harpsichord with organ pipes.

Berlin, Staatliche Musikinstrumenten-Sammlung (Catalogue by Curt Sachs, No. 2609).

194

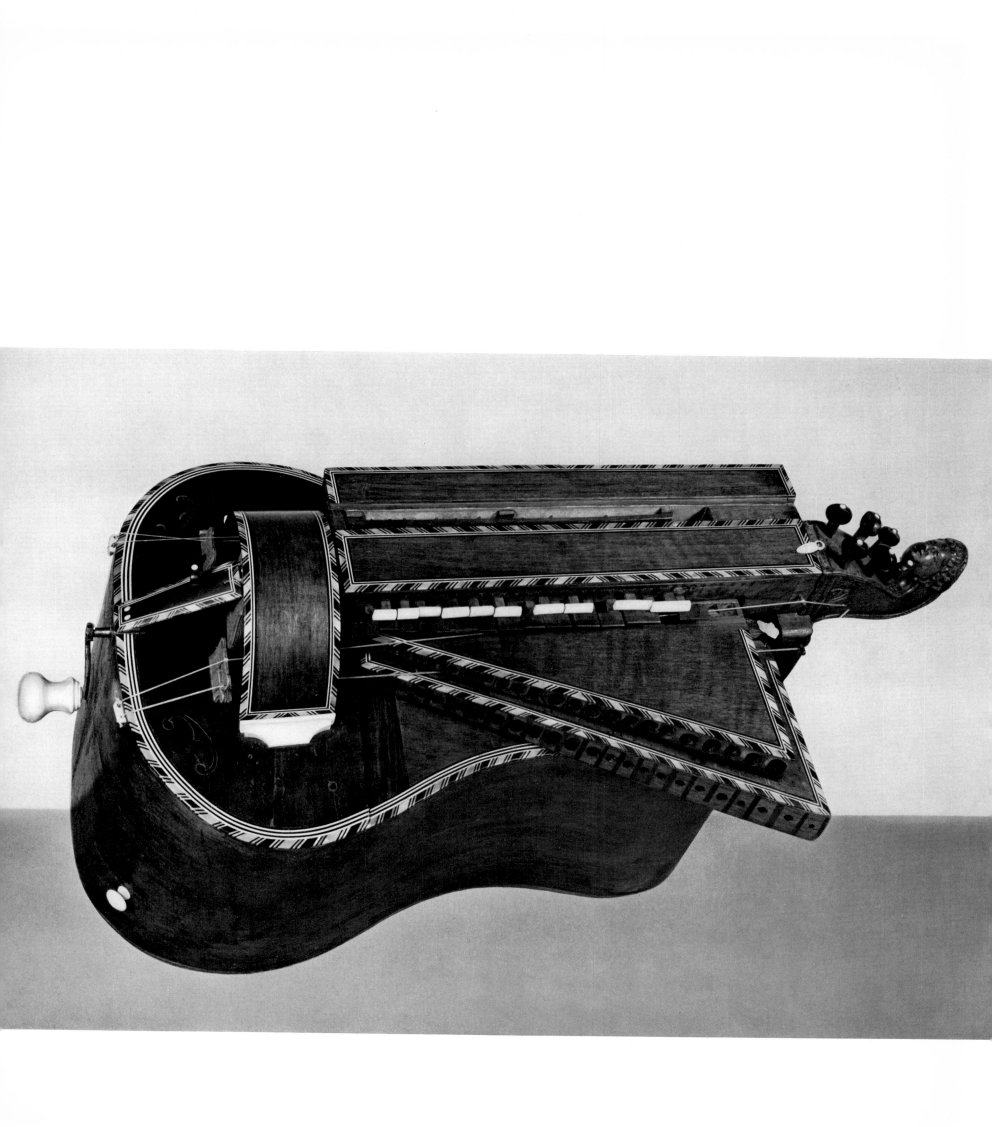

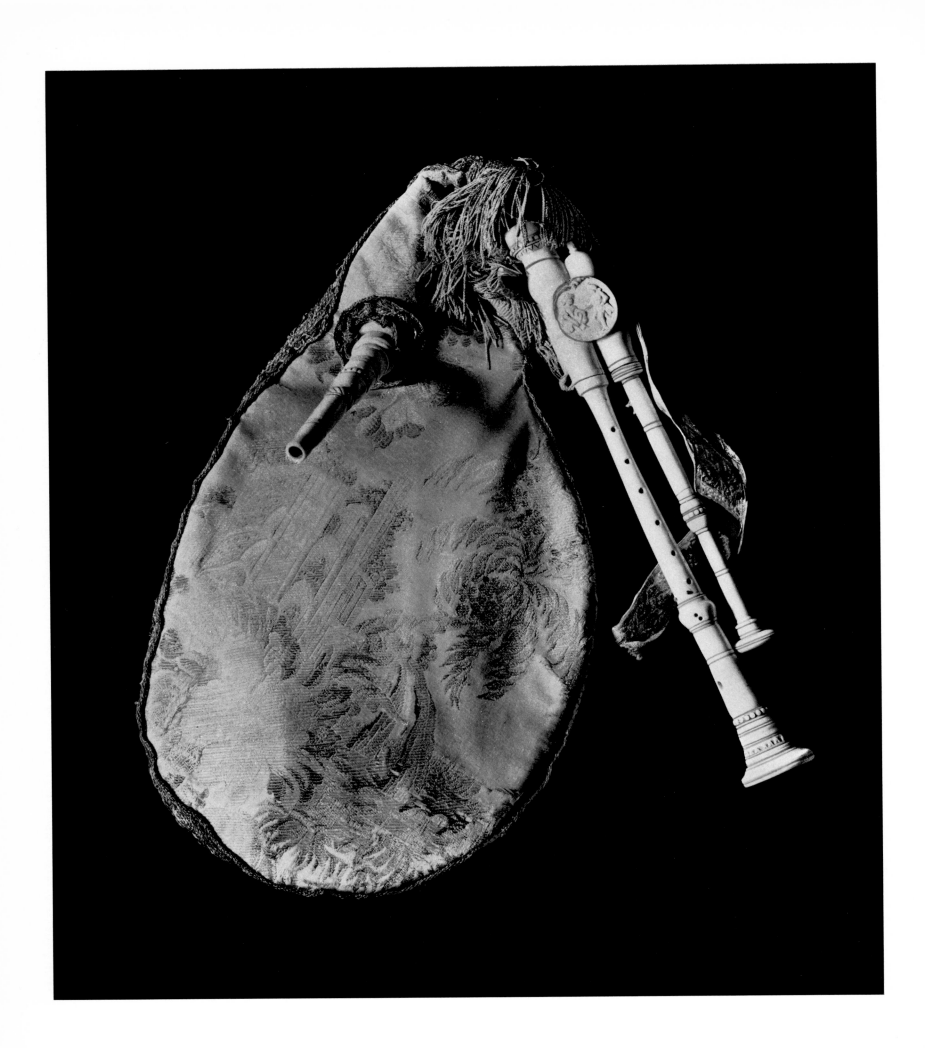

75 *Cornemuse*

France, 18th century

Like the hurdy-gurdy (Pl. 73), the bagpipe (see Pl. 76) became an important tool and requisite of the pastoral fashion, especially in France. As a rule, the bagpipes used in the *Fêtes Champêtres* were ladies' instruments such as the musette, a small and dainty instrument furnished with bellows, which replaced the blowpipe—the playing of which caused a puffing up of the player's cheeks in a manner unbecoming to court ladies. But also simpler forms with blowpipes were used, such as the cornemuse illustrated here. Its short blowpipe is of ivory, as is the stock, and, emerging from it, the chanter and the single small dronepipe. The chanter has six finger holes in front and one behind, and a lower hole stopped by a silver key.

The bag is covered with silk tapestry and bordered with gold and silver lace. An ivory plaquette on the stock shows a girl and a boy in pseudo-rustic garb. Tassels and ribbons complete the gay picture.

New York, Metropolitan Museum of Art, 89.4.865 (Crosby Brown Collection 1889).

76 *Bock*

German, 18th century

In its simplest form, the bagpipe consists of (a) a bag, (b) a short blowpipe through which the player inflates the bag with air, and (c) one or more reed pipes through which the air leaves the bag, thus producing sound. The bag, which serves as a flexible wind reservoir, is made of the skin or bladder of an animal, usually a goat or sheep; the pipes are inserted into the natural holes of the skin (where the animal's neck or feet had been), by means of cylinders of wood (the so-called stocks) round which the skin is tightly fastened with a cord. The blowpipe, where it enters the bag, is fitted with a leather flap valve that prevents the air from passing back. The sounding pipes—primitive oboes or clarinets—differ in structure and function. One, called the chanter, is fitted with finger holes that shorten the vibrating air column within the pipe and thus permit the playing of a melody. The other, which is usually larger, has no finger holes and is therefore capable of only one tone – the continuous and invariable bass called the drone (a name also given to this pipe). The playing position of the bagpipe is well known: the player holds the blowpipe in his mouth, fingers the chanter in front of him like an oboe or clarinet, and squeezes the bag under one of his arms, thus regulating the air pressure.

Like so many instruments, the bagpipe came to Europe from Asia, and was known already in ancient Rome: Martial mentions the bagpipe; and Nero, contrary to popular belief, did not

POLNISCHER BOCK.

*Ich bin ein schöner Mensch und kan so trefflich pfeiffen
auf den anmuthigen Bock, daß manchen übel wird:
auch! wie die Bären selbst ein Menuet begreiffen,
Doch weil von vieler Müh der Hals gantz abgekirrt
so schenckt ihr Tantzende, die trotz den Bären springen
mir bald was in den Bock: so will ich lustig singen.*

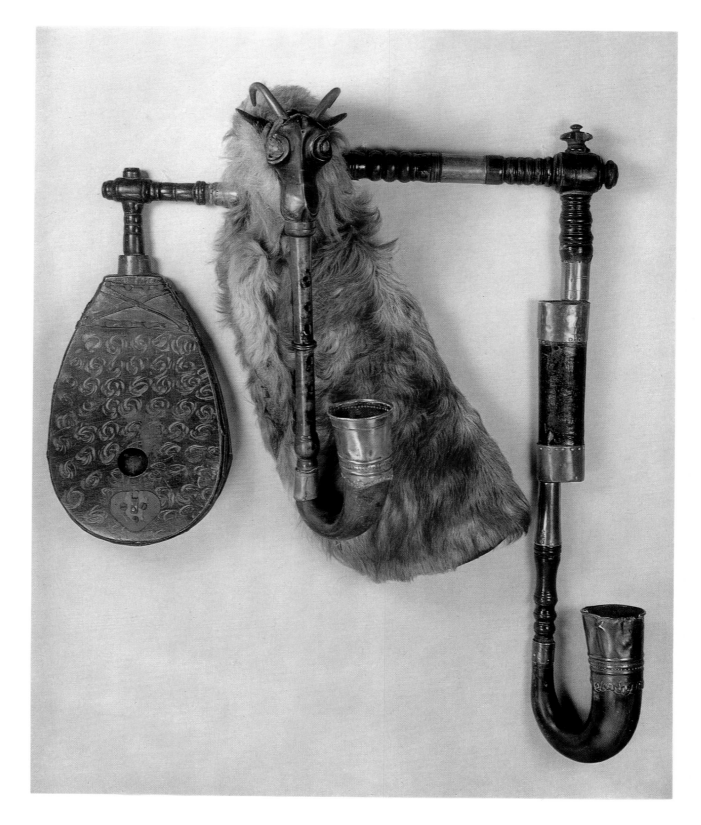

78 _Transverse Flute with extra joints and quiver box_

France, mid-18th century

Square box with various joints of a transverse flute

France, second half of 18th century

Flute cases were made in various forms: besides the flat Case, round quiver-shaped boxes were used, and also bulky square boxes with separate holes for each joint and an oblique cover to accommodate joints of different length.

According to tradition, the complete one-key transverse flute in the foreground was used by Frederick the Great.

Berlin, Staatliche Musikinstrumentensammlung No. 4229. The flute box at the left is there on permanent loan.

79 *Violin Case*

Germany, 18th century

Instrument cases are even rarer than old instruments. In paintings with *Fêtes Champêtres*, in Dutch genre scenes, and in Lombard still lifes one occasionally observes a lute case or the awkward chest for a whole set of recorders or transverse flutes; but very few such boxes have come down to us, even if the instruments themselves survived. The present rococo case surely owes its survival to its visual charm. Unlike the modern practical violin cases, this protective shell tries to simulate pliability and to follow like a skin the shape of the treasure it houses. The box and the lid are each carved of one piece. The carving is exquisite. Gilded rocailles with leaves and flowers overgrow head, tail end, and the side walls. A rounded medallion with initials, probably those of the owner, decorates the center, and the remaining sections are decorated with rich clusters of musical instruments and music books.

New York, Metropolitan Museum of Art, 52.96.2. Purchase, 1952.

80 **Cane Flute (Recorder)**
Pressburg, c. 1800. Signed: "F. Scholnast, Presburg"

Cane Violin
Germany, 19th century

Cane Clarinet
Paris, 19th century. Signed: "Henri Pourcelle, Paris"

Cane Flutes (Recorders) and Cane Violin
Possibly German, c. 1800

Cane violins and other instruments made in the shape of walking sticks were popular, especially in Germany, from the last decades of the eighteenth century until well into the Biedermeier period. The Sentimental Age must have been very fond of musical instruments that helped the romantic wayfarer to respond immediately to experiences such as seeing a beautiful sunset or hearing the nocturnal whispering of the trees.

The cane violin was invented after the middle of the eighteenth century by Johann Wilde, a German musician at the imperial court of St. Petersburg. The hollow body of the cane serves as a resonator. When closed, the instrument is a walking stick with a handle. For playing, the handle could be unscrewed, the cover lid of the body removed, the bow taken out of its repository inside the violin body, the handle screwed on again to serve as a chin rest, and the little bridge raised; the violin was then ready for playing. The belly of the violin here has two long, flame-shaped sound holes. Since there is no neck or scroll with pegs, the strings are attached to little metal screws which can be wound with a clock key.

Simpler in construction were the various woodwind instruments built in this walking-stick fashion: vertical and transverse flutes, and even clarinets. These instruments flourished in Germany and Austria (the idea of making them originated in Bohemia), along with the cane violin, during the early part of the nineteenth century. The cane violin had a local renascence in Vienna at the end of that century.

New York, Metropolitan Museum of Art, 89.4.930, 89.4.928, 89.4.950, 89.4.2165 (Crosby Brown Collection, 1889); 46.34.60, 46.34.72 (gift of Miss Alice Getty, 1946). Background: 41.100.297, side chair of painted and gilded walnut, Italian, 3rd quarter of the 18th century (gift of George Blumenthal, 1941).

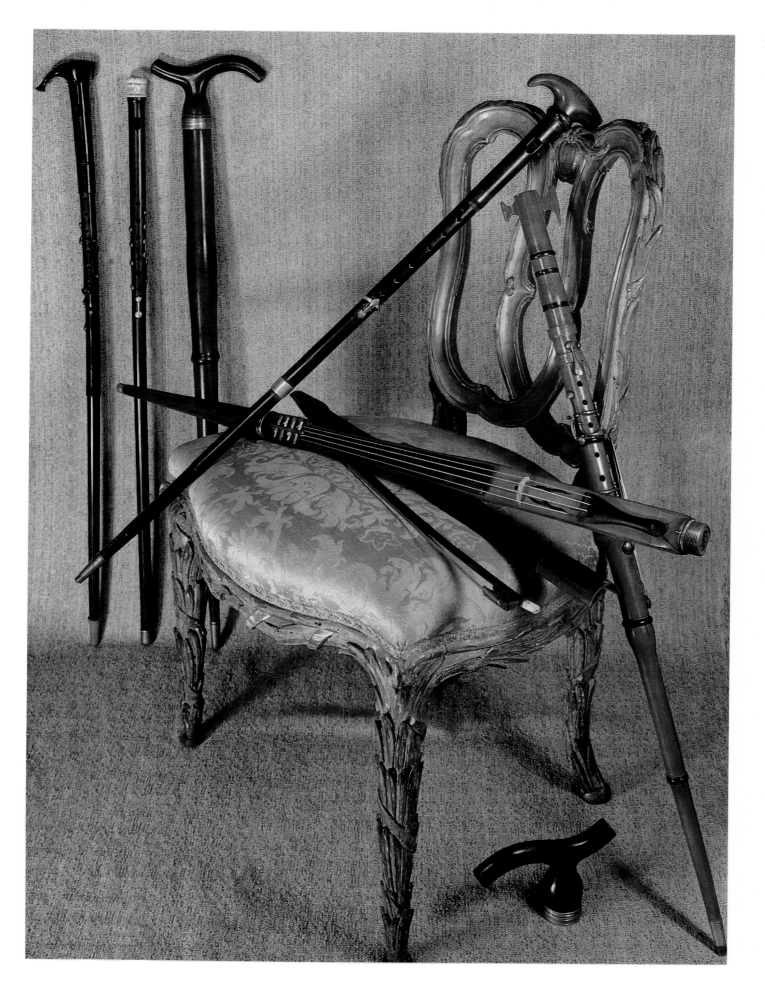

81 *Walking-Stick Violin*

About 1810

This typical Biedermeier piece is richly decorated with inlay of bone and mother-of-pearl.
The removable cover (shown at the left) and the lower end of the stick itself have geometrical
patterns; the stick handle shows a floral design.
Instead of pegs there are four tuning screws of metal.
Munich, Städtische Instrumentensammlung, No. 41/302.

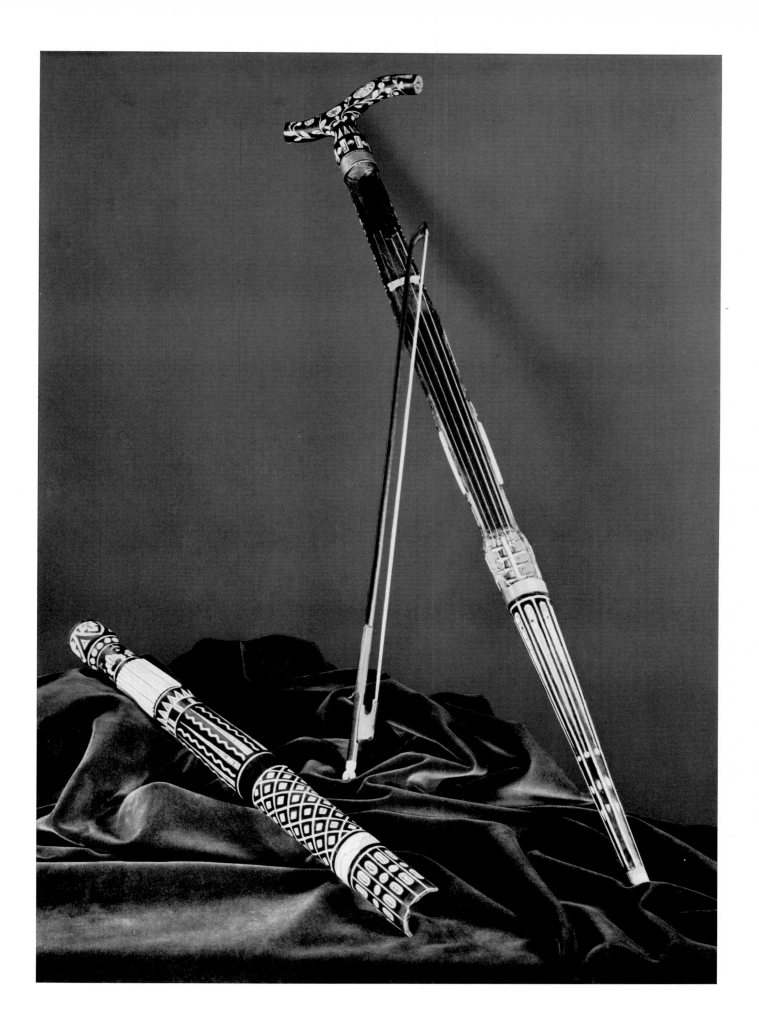

HARFFENIST.

Was Harffenklang vermag kan David bestens zeigen
mit seinem Nebalim: und richtig wer versteht,
was Geist und Ohr ergötzt kan hier das Ziel erreichen
wornach sein Hertze tracht und sein verlangen geht
drum bleibt diß meine Lust: weil ich mit diesen Saiten
mein gantzes All vergnüg zu gut und bösen Zeiten

82 *Hooked Harp*

Austrian (probably), 18th century

For many centuries of European music, the harp with a diatonic row of strings (no semitones) served its purpose well: each string sounded its full length and no shortening or stopping of the strings was required, nor was it technically feasible on this instrument. Only in the sixteenth century did the increasing use of chromatic tones make composers and instrument builders look for new solutions. Monteverdi's "Orfeo" already used an *arpa doppia*, which had a second set of strings to supply the accidentals. But the great size and awkward playing technique seems to have made this solution a very problematic one. An easier and more ingenious answer to the problem was found in the second half of the seventeenth century, in the Tyrol: the hooked harp (Hakenharfe). Metal hooks were inserted into the neck of the harp, close to the upper end of each string. When the player turned the hook, the corresponding string was shortened, and the pitch thus raised by a semitone.

This hooked harp of the eighteenth century, probably Austrian, is one of the most beautiful examples of this type. The three basic elements—sound box, neck, and pillar—accept quite different degrees of decoration. The sound box, in order not to be deadened by heavy ornamentation, is embellished only by nine small mock sound holes with a fine hexagonal star design set in. The pillar too is rather plain, a very narrow strip of the wood running its entire length, simply carved. The neck alone, with its complex curvature necessitated by the grading of the strings (and thus by a functional requirement), is a feast for the eye. Here a veritable profusion of decoration, a feast of rococo forms, materializes. The neck springs in a slender curve from the upper end of the sound box and, gradually increasing in width, makes possible scrolls and terminates in a stunning climax: the figure of a richly costumed boy playing a transverse flute. It seems as if the whole harp, whose nature it is to play chords and passage work, suggests here the solo player whose melody it is supposed to accompany.

New York, Metropolitan Museum of Art, 58.150 (purchase, Rogers Fund, 1958). Background: 41.100.297, side chair of painted and gilded walnut, Italian, 3rd quarter of the 18th century (gift of George Blumenthal, 1941).

83 *Baryton (Viola di Bordone)*

by Daniel Achatius Stadlmann, Vienna, 1732
Signed: "Daniel Achatius Stadlmann, Lauten- und Geigenmacher in Wienn, anno 1732"

The baryton, with its six gut strings, is actually a bass *viola da gamba*. However, in addition to the gut strings, it has, like the *viola d'amore*, a number of sympathetic metal strings that, if tuned appropriately, respond "sympathetically" to the sound of the gut strings. In the baryton the sympathetic strings also have a second function: they can be reached by the player's left thumb at the rear of the broad neck and thus add their silvery plucked tone to that of the bowed gut strings. The technique required is difficult and seems to have prevented a widespread use of the instrument. It was used chiefly in South Germany and Austria, but it had a remarkably long life, from the end of the seventeenth century until well into the middle of the nineteenth century. Its peak was in the second half of the eighteenth century. Joseph Haydn's patron, Prince Nikolaus Esterhazy, was an expert performer on the baryton, and Haydn wrote for him no less than 175 compositions for this instrument, exploiting its tonal possibilities with inexhaustible imagination.

Because of the enormous pull of the many strings, barytons were often equipped with metal bars to reinforce the wooden body; but the builder of the instrument shown here managed to do without them. This baryton has the deep body of a bass gamba. The slightly arched belly is perforated by a double pair of sound holes of flame shape, and has a large number of small auxiliary bridges for the sympathetic strings, in addition to the large bridge for the gut strings. There are seven movable frets. A beautiful, large pegbox carries sixteen pegs. To its back is attached a small pegbox in fine carving, with four pegs. The carved and painted head with its feathered hat that crowns the neck, the complex outline of the body, and the elegant inlay of ivory and ebony decorating the finger board and string holder, all add to the distinction of this masterpiece.

Kunsthistorisches Museum, Vienna. Property of the Gesellschaft der Musikfreunde, No. 46 (inventory of the collection by E. Mandyczewski); donated by Jos. Reich in 1838, according to whose information the instrument had been part of the estate of Joseph Haydn. Background: Oesterreichisches Museum für angewandte Kunst, Vienna – T 8696, large bed cover, yellow-green damask, Italian, ca 1700. Chair: property of the Kunsthistorisches Museum, Vienna.

214

84 *Violin*

made of tortoise shell, by Wenzel Kowansky, Prague, 1749

The body of this unique instrument is made entirely of tortoise shell; the purflings of the soundboard and those of the back are of gold. Neck, finger board, and string holder are of ivory and inlaid with tortoise shell and gold. A little carved ivory head, complete with wig, crowns the pegbox. However, the ivory bridge is not the original one for the instrument.

The beautiful ivory bow was made at the same time as the instrument and is in the same style, its top carved in the shape of a dragon's head. It is elegantly fluted, with inlays of tortoise shell and gold.

Sammlung alter Musikinstrumente, Kunsthistorisches Museum, Vienna (Schlosser Catalogue No. S. 100). Background: Oesterreichisches Museum für Angewandte Kunst, Vienna, T 9058 –Part of a bed canopy, silk-damask, first half, 18th century, from T 6090 –White batiste handkerchief, Austrian, mid-19th century.

85 *Organ*

in the Grote Kerk dedicated to St. Bavo, Haarlem
Built by Christian Mulder, 1735–1738

To perceive the radical change in the prevailing style of organ building, it is rewarding to compare this illustration with that in Plate 29. It is not so much the difference between southern and northern tradition that is important here, but rather the contrast between a quiet, classical, well-proportioned design and a dramatic, dynamic, upsurging form that offers the beholder not one but a whole series of different aspects.

Here, in the famous Grote Kerk in Haarlem, it is Gothic space that surrounds a late Baroque organ. The organ prospect, which towers high, almost to the rib vault, receives magnificent, dramatic light from the ogival windows. The whole design is dominated by "bass towers," that is, groups of bass pipes that are bundled together into something like Gothic composite pillars. Such projecting bass towers had already been employed in French organs of the late Renaissance (for instance, in St. Maclou, Rouen, 1520–1542; Notre Dame, Alençon, 1537; Caudebec, Caux, 1542; the Cathedral of Chartres, 1545–1551), and also in Holland (in the large organ built in the Oude Kerk in Amsterdam, 1540–1545). But in all these examples the organs rose from the same horizontal platform, animating and enriching the relief of the drospect but not its basic contour. In St. Bavo, however, the bass towers not only create a forceful, varied relief and a dramatic articulation of light and shadow, but they rise from levels of different height: the flanking ones from a lower, the central one from a much higher level thus imparting to the whole prospect a strong upward surge like a giant hand with many fingers pointing towards heaven. One important result of the strong and complex relief is that the organ offers the visitor not one but many views, merging into each other as he approaches or moves across the church from left to right. The observer of detail will notice that the smaller pipes that form the rear plane of the prospect are also organized around a bundle of pipes which, however, are not in the form of a round, engaged column but of a square pillar with a projecting edge.

All this play with convex and concave forms, all this undulating relief, is reflected and summed up as it were by the broken cornice connecting at the top all the bundles of pipes, and rising and falling in harmony with the different levels from which the pipes spring. It is no doubt this upward surge—sensual as well as symbolical—that makes this work of the late Baroque admirably fit its Gothic environment.

The design of the main prospect, contour as well as relief, is repeated in diminution (to borrow a musical term) in the small organ beneath it, the so-called "Rückpositif."

The whole structure is crowned by the coat of arms of the city of Haarlem, with the inscription "VICIT VIM VIRTUS"; the flanking bass towers are topped by statues of King David and an allegory of sacred music not to mention the many other allegorical figures decorating the structure.

87 *Harpsichord*

by Johannes Goermans, Paris, 1754, converted into a pianoforte
Inscribed: "IOANNES GOERMANS ME FECIT PARISIS 1754"

This beautiful instrument is a living document of an important transition in the history of keyboard instruments marked by the ascendency of the pianoforte over the harpsichord. The instrument was built as a double manual harpsichord, but later, probably towards the end of the eighteenth century, was converted into a pianoforte, a procedure that of course necessitated replacing quill-bearing jacks by hammers. Actually, the jacks remained in place in this instrument, but instead of carrying quills, they serve as dampers. The deeply recessed space in the front, which contained both keyboards, is now only partly filled by one. Originally there must have been several stops; and, indeed, a close inspection of the soundboard confirms this. Today it has only one bridge, over which triple strings are carried; but a curved double line in blue, crossing the soundboard in a space left free by the flower decoration, marks precisely the place where a second bridge, for the four-foot stop, was fastened. Actually, behind this line can be detected traces of the holes for the hitch pins to which the four-foot strings were attached. Thus it appears that the original mechanism had one four-foot and at least one, probably two, eight-foot stops.

The decoration is of great distinction, and shows a pleasant blending of Flemish and French styles. The soundboard, in typically Flemish manner, is painted with flowers and birds; the sound hole is adorned with a medallion of pewter, showing, as the instruments in the Ruckers' tradition do, the initials of the maker flanking an allegorical figure, in this case an angel playing a harp. The lid and the walls of the case – there is no outer case such as the Italian harpsichords have – are also lavishly decorated: the outside with musical trophies and floral ornaments, the inside of the lid with black and gold *chinoiseries*, groups of musicians playing various instruments, and bird and flower designs, against a brilliant red background. Around the lady playing a two-bank harpsichord, in decorative detail very like our instrument, we find a recorder player and two musicians with viols; the one with the *viola da gamba* holds his bow in the characteristic position, palm upward.

Johannes Goermans was of Flemish origin and retained many elements of the Flemish harpsichord tradition. However, during the second part of the eighteenth century he worked in Paris, where he died in 1777.

New York, Metropolitan Museum of Art, 44.157.8. Anonymous gift, 1944.

88 *Clavicytherium*

by Martin Kaiser, Austria, end of the 17th century
Inscribed: "Martinus Kaiser Ser. Electoris Palatini Instrumentorum Opifex et huiusmodi
Inventor"

This instrument is, in its simple and harmonious proportions, a masterpiece of architectural
furniture. The decoration, applied with elegant restraint, consists of turtle shell, mother-of-
pearl, and ebony inlays, and gilded appliqués. The lower keys are covered with turtle shell,
the upper ones with mother-of-pearl. On the front panel of the base the Austrian double
eagle is shown.
This clavicytherium was built for Emperor Leopold I, whose reign lasted from 1658 to 1705.
The four little legs are later additions. The instrument is the only extant work of Martin
Kaiser, who worked in Füssen, Allgäu.
Sammlung alter Musikinstrumente, Kunsthistorisches Museum, Vienna (No. 377–8801).

226

89 **Harp**

France, 18th century

This amusing monster is the creation of piscatorial fantasy. Sound box and neck are formed by the round body and tail of a whale; the pillar has the shape of a harpoon. Teeth, tongue, and the ornamental suggestion of eyes contribute to the jocular realism. This eighteenth century example of zoomorphism in instrument building must have been made for a special purpose, perhaps a spectacle or theatrical performance or a jolly reunion of fishermen.
Kunsthistorisches Museum, Vienna. Eigentum der Gesellschaft der Musikfreunde, No. 84.

90 *Pedal Harp (single action)*

by Jean Henry Naderman (père), Paris, 18th century

Naderman père was the founder of a celebrated dynasty of instrument makers, harpists, and publishers in Paris. He was in the royal service, and this harp was owned by Marie Antoinette. Its decoration is a veritable dictionary of Louis XVI decor. The pillar, whose surface is completely encased in flat gilded leaves, has in addition a gilded garland of flowers wound around it in a long spiral. Even richer is the carving at the top of the pillar and the base of the instrument:—a large golden eagle is perched under a leaf spiral at the top; and putti, riding on sea horses and blowing conch shells, below. Gilded leaves also cover the rim of the neck. Only the sound box does not carry the prevailing, gilded-leaf decoration, since it could not resonate properly under such heavy ornamentation. However, it is lavishly painted with representations of flower garlands, musical instruments, and fountains with dolphins.

The firm of Naderman was famous for single-action harps, whose pedals, by means of wires concealed in the pillar, could turn hooks fixed in the neck and thereby tighten the strings to sound a semitone higher. J. H. Naderman waged a literary feud against his competitor, Sébastian Erard, who produced double-action harps that facilitated the raising of pitch of the strings by another semitone.

Paris, Musée Instrumental du Conservatoire National de Musique, E 482. C293. Gift of Baronne Dornier.

91 *Lyre Guitars*

Gennaro Fabricatore, Naples, 1807
Lupot, Orleans, 1778
Salomon, Paris, early 19th century

In the Napoleonic era, a ladies' instrument, the lyre guitar, became fashionable throughout Europe. It was a guitar in lyre shape: more precisely, the neck and the stopped strings of a true guitar were combined for the sake of appearance with the arms and the crossbar of an ancient Greek or Roman lyre. But now the crossbar carried no open strings; and, in fact, the technique remained that of stopping strings against a finger board as in lutes, guitars, violins, etc. However, the appearance was immensely attractive, and the elegant shape, borrowed from antiquity, harmonized well with the flowing garb of the ladies at the courts of Vienna, Milan, and Naples, in Regency London, and in the Paris Directoire.

However, this revival of an ancient and venerable shape in the early nineteenth century was by no means the first one. It was already known in the Carolingian renaissance, and the beautiful illustrations of the ninth century Utrecht Psalter show lyre guitars side by side with true Roman lyres and kitharas. Much later, in the Italian Renaissance, there was again a revival of the ancient forms, this time under the impact of newly restored or excavated ancient statuary and sarcophagi. We find lyre guitars then in the hands of angels, in sacred paintings, and as attributes of allegorical figures. From that time on, throughout the Baroque and Rococo era, the ancient form as a decorative element never disappeared. And one can hardly imagine a Vienna Biedermeier home without the lyre guitar. It was even used by celebrated *Lieder* singers of the time, such as Schubert's friend, Johann Michael Vogl, for performing compositions to classical texts.

New York, Metropolitan Museum of Art, 89.4.1056, 89.4.2590, 89.4.1071 (Crosby Brown Collection, 1889).

92 *Harp-Lyre*

Italy, 19th century. Signed: "Carlo Scalfi"

The Greek revival period, which produced lyre-guitars, also indulged in several different forms all patterned more or less on the shape of the Greek kithara. One of them, a piece which is probably unique, is the harp-lyre shown here, an instrument lavishly decorated with elements derived from the classical revival of the early nineteenth century.

The body of the instrument, resting on its own small base, is wide and bulky. The yoke and the kithara arms, terminating in two round plaques decorated with representations of the sun and moon, are of course nonfunctional. The soundboard is furnished with thirty-two double strings; twenty-six of them are attached to a diagonal row of tuning pins and run over one long bridge and then down over two shorter bridges which are placed lower on the soundboard. In addition there are six double bass strings which run from tuning pins on the moon plaque down over another short bridge at the lower part of the soundboard. The twenty-six melody strings are equipped with little metal hooks for raising their pitch by a semitone, similar to the mechanism of a hooked harp. The soundboard, with its border of inlaid mother-of-pearl and three sound holes, has a profusion of miniature paintings on it showing angels, musicians, flowers, and butterflies. The instrument has the name of Carlo Scalfi prominently set forth both on the large platform pedestal and on the small base.

The platform pedestal rests on lions' feet and is decorated with Roman profiles and carved gilt leaves. Its use here, too, harks back to ancient models: many Roman sarcophagi with Muses show kitharas on pedestals. The most striking features of this pedestal are the massive, gilded, winged sphinxes that flank the sides of the sound box. They did not, as it might at first appear, hamper the motion of the player's arms, since the whole instrument can be removed from its Greek-revival setting by turning a metal screw in the base of the lyre. Thus the instrument was not merely a showpiece, a fact which is also evident from the existence of the rather intricate hook mechanism.

New York, Metropolitan Museum of Art, 11.68.2 (Gift of Mr. and Mrs. William H. Herriman, 1911).

93 *Basset Horns*

German, ca. 1800

Basset horns have nothing to do with horns; they are alto clarinets with a longer tube, narrower bore, and thinner wall than the regular clarinet. To reduce their length, in order to facilitate holding and playing these instruments, they were built in curved or angled shapes and had a box (in German, *"Buch"* – book – or *"Kasten"*) in which the tube is doubled back twice before expanding into the metal bell. The invention of the basset horn, in about 1770, is credited to an instrument maker by the name of Mayrhofer who worked in Passau, Bavaria. Towards 1800, the preferred shape consisted of two straight joints meeting at a wide angle and held together by a short knee joint of ivory, horn, or wood. It is this angular shape that gives these basset horns their curious, unforgettable appearance reminiscent of certain insect legs, reinforced at the knees.

The tone of the basset horn is sombre, sad, and velvety. E. T. A. Hoffmann, the Romantic poet, painter, composer, and music critic, compared its sound to the perfume of carnations. It was Mozart, above all composers – with his continuous interest in new timbres – who employed the basset horn for solemn and melancholy effects. He used it in his Gran Partita for twelve wind instruments and contrabass (KV 361), later in *La Clemenza di Tito*, *The Magic Flute*, the *Requiem*, and also in the *Adagio* (KV 411) in which three basset horns are combined with a pair of regular clarinets. In much of Mozart's masonic music, the solemn passages are entrusted to the basset horn. Beethoven and Mendelssohn used the basset horn occasionally; Richard Strauss revived it with great success in *Electra*, *Der Rosenkavalier*, and *Die Frau ohne Schatten*.

New York, Metropolitan Museum of Art. 89.4.1560, 89.4.1387, 89.4.2143 (Crosby Brown Collection, 1889); 53.56.12 – gift of the University Museum, University of Pennsylvynia, 1953. Background: 59.191.3 – Cloth: chiné à la branche plain cloth, French, 18th century, gift of Mrs. Orme Wilson, 1959.

94 *Slide Trombones, Tenor in B flat*

Italian, early 19th century
Belgian, early 19th century
French, early 19th century

Animal shapes have often been exploited in the decoration of musical instruments. In the Orient we find the peacock lutes of India, the bat (a sign bringing luck) on Chinese and Japanese lutes, the crocodile cither of Burma, the Chinese slit drum in the form of a wooden fish, and many others.

In the Occident, serpent and dragon heads were often used, their shape lending itself perfectly to the decoration of the bells of both woodwind and brass instruments. The beautiful miniatures in the Cantigas de Santa Maria of Alfonso the Wise of Castile, the richest collection of popular Spanish music of the thirteenth century, contain outstanding examples illustrating the use of human and animal heads on instruments. (Vignette.)

In the Renaissance, this picturesque use played an important role in the fantastic instruments used on the stage (vignette) in various spectacles. Sometimes even violins were disguised as serpents, such as those played by allegorical figures in a performance staged in Florence in 1565 for the wedding of Francesco dei Medici and Giovanna of Austria. In this, as in many other cases, the animal shape carried with it a symbolic significance.

Such bizarre shapes were carried over into the Baroque and, for public occasions, for instance in military bands, even into the nineteenth century. The instruments shown here are military slide trombones. The lower end of the tubes gradually widen, assuming reptile scales and terminating in dragon heads with wide-open mouths. The instrument in the middle even has a flickering tongue, moved by the air stream issuing from the bell.

New York Metropolitan Museum of Art, 89.4.1301, 89.4.2408, 89.4.2152 (Crosby Brown Collection, 1889).

95 *Ophicleide, Bass in B flat*

European, c. 1825

The ophicleide, actually a low bugle with keys, comes as the end of a long development which began in the Renaissance with the cornetto (a wooden pipe, often covered with leather, that had side holes like a flute but had a cup-shaped mouthpiece like a brass instrument). When bass instruments of similar timbre were needed, the serpent was developed, whose undulating

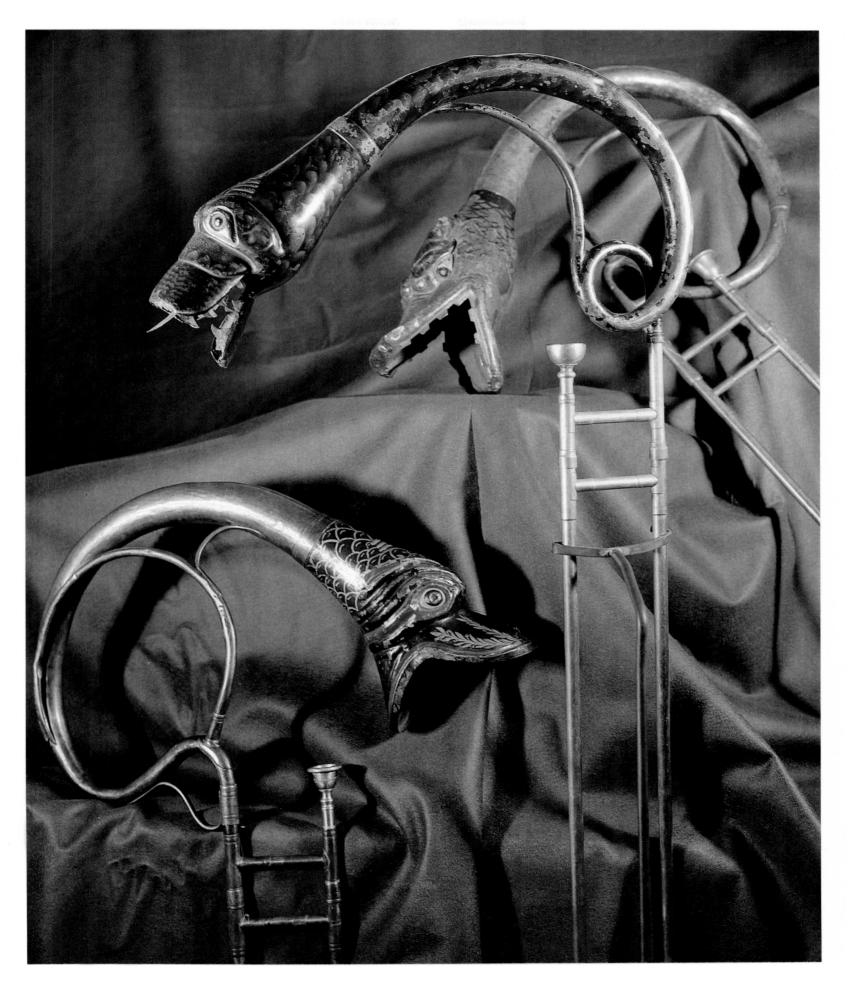

shape made it possible to reach its finger holes in spite of its ungainly size. Still later, the double bent shape of the bassoon was found more practical, and the bass horn developed which had a wooden bassoonlike tube, keys, and a cup-shaped mouthpiece. The replacement of the wooden tube by metal finally led to the creation of the ophicleide, in France in 1817.

The new instrument was a triumphant success in Spontini's *Olympia* (1819), and quickly became indispensable in opera and symphony orchestras and military bands. After 1840, it yielded to the tuba in Germany, but held its own much longer in France, Italy, and South America. Its name, from ὄφίς (serpent) and κλεῖς (key)—meaning keyed serpent—was characteristic of a time in which hardly a year passed without new patents for musical instruments under fancy Greek or Latin names.

New York, Metropolitan Museum of Art, 89.4.2564 (Crosby Brown Collection, 1889).

96 *Clarinet in B flat*

by Charles Joseph Sax (1791–1865), Brussels, 1830

The clarinet, a comparatively recent member of the orchestra, was used in its early years by Rameau, Gluck, and, in full and ingenious exploitation of its wide and varied range, by Mozart. From Beethoven's time on, a pair of clarinets in the orchestra has been indispensable. It is not without interest that an imaginative orchestrator like Berlioz should ascribe to its timbre (in his *Grand traité d'instrumentation et d'orchestration modernes*, Paris, 1844) two quite different and hardly compatible emotional qualities. At one point he calls it an epic instrument whose voice is that of heroic love and little fit for idylls. Yet when he comes to describe its role in Weber's opera *Der Freischütz*, he gives a long and ecstatic description of the dreamy melody of the clarinet, characterizing the lonesome maiden—the tender lamentation of the blonde bride of the sharpshooter, with her eyes toward heaven.

Ivory clarinets are rare; some were made as early as the eighteenth century, but ivory, apart from its high cost, has often been found less satisfactory in timbre than wood. There is no denying its beauty, however. The clarinet shown here, decorated with the arms of the Princes of Orange and Counts of Nassau, is of exceptional loveliness, its tube of ivory, mountings and keys of golden, mellow brass engraved with leaf designs, and key covers embossed in the shape of lions' heads. The instrument is inscribed on the bell, below the coat of arms: "*C. Sax/ Facteur du Roi/à Bruxelles.*" It was Charles Sax, father of Adolph Sax, who helped to establish the tradition of fine craftsmanship in making wind instruments which was continued by his son, by Mahillon, and other makers and inventors in Brussels.

New York, Metropolitan Museum of Art, 53.223.

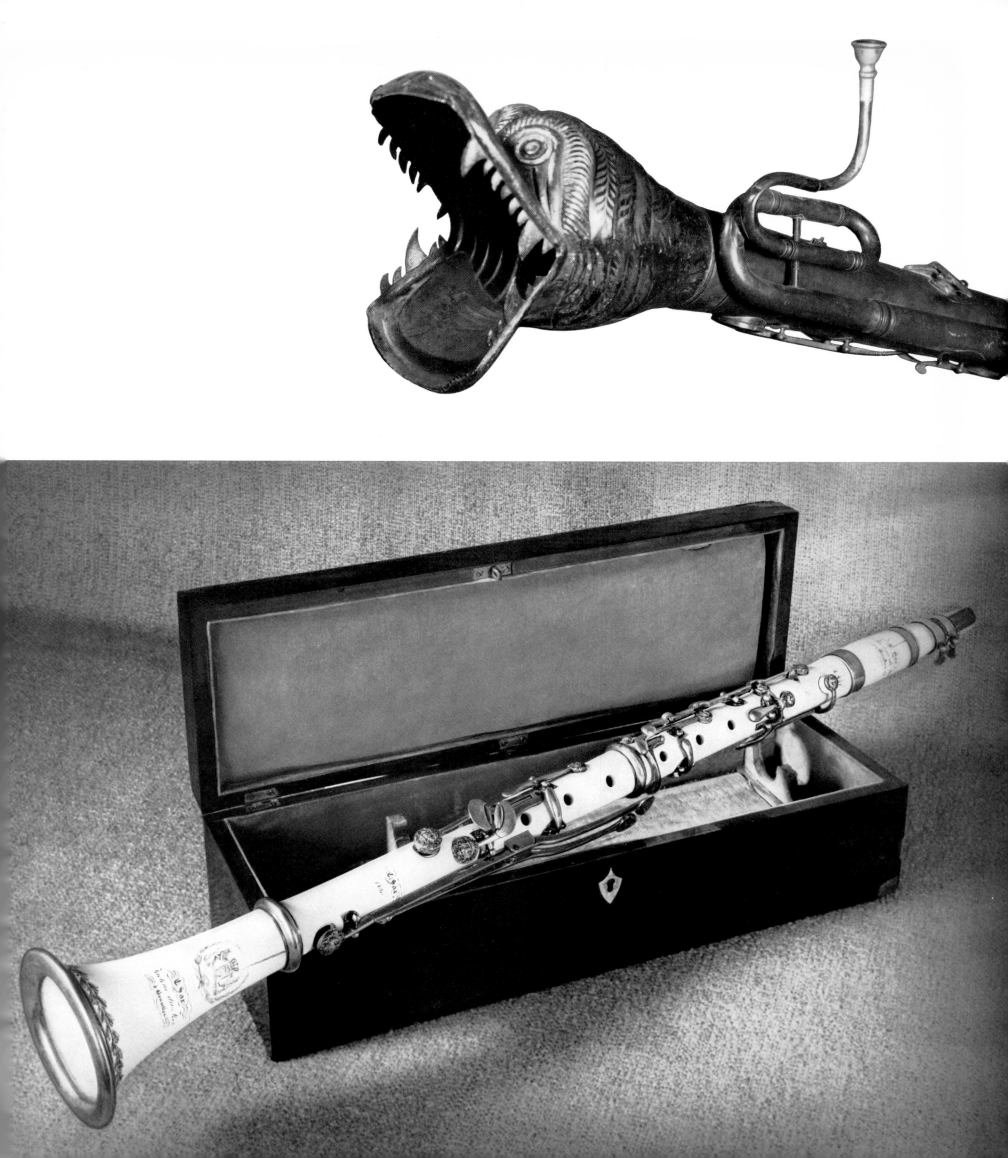

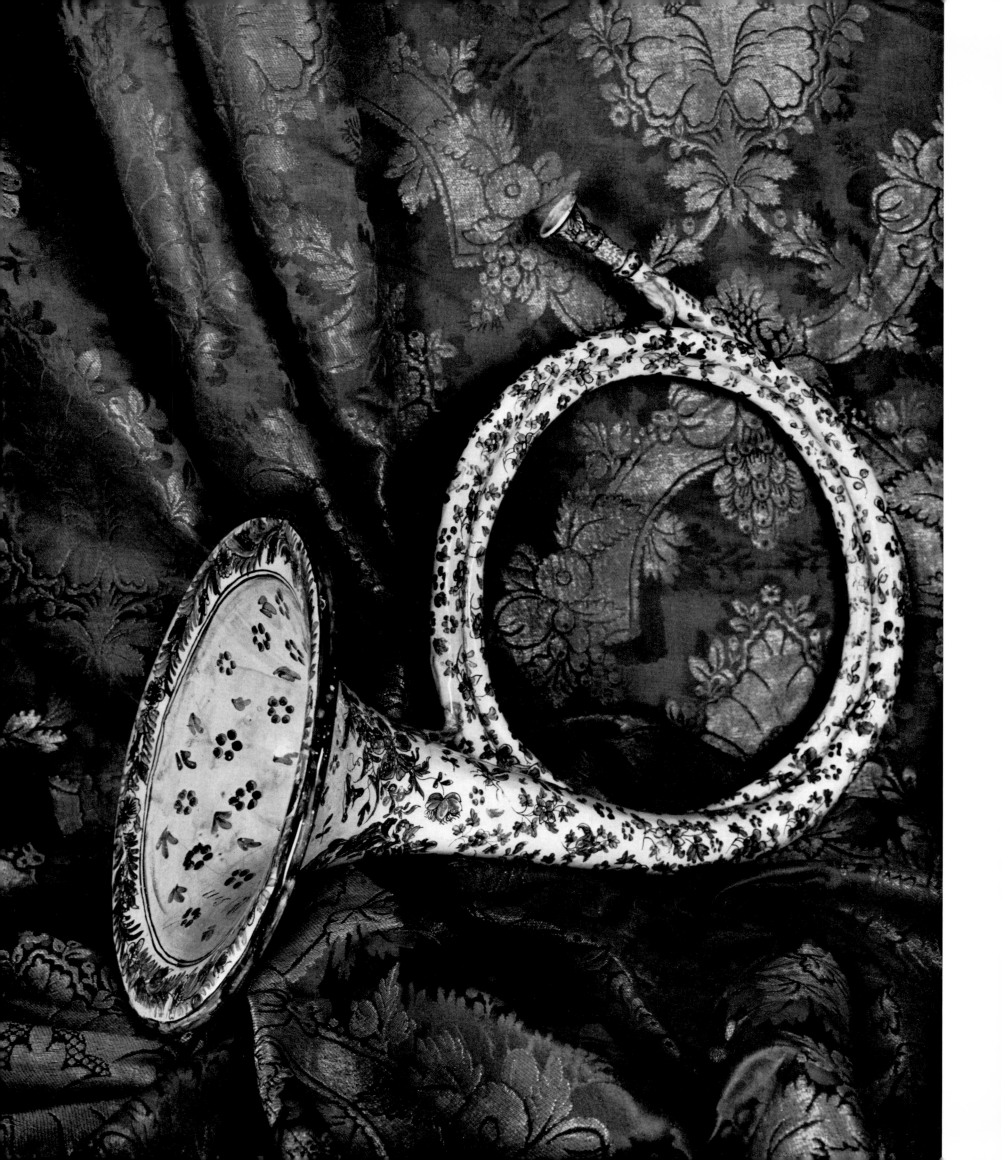

WALDHORN

Es ist nicht leicht ein Fürst der meine Kunst nichtachtet
vielmehr an jeden Hof wird sie aufs höchst geliebt.
wañ man den schüchtern Wild in grünen Wald nachtrachtet
und dem erhitzten Schwein ein kaltes Eißen gibt
so wird von meinen Horn das Hertz in Muth gesetzet
auch hält man kein Festin da nicht mein Mund ergötzet.

97 *Horn in G*

German, 18th century

The widely flaring bell and the simple, circular form of cylindrical tube characterized a variety
of related horns often associated with the sport of hunting: Jagdhorn, Waldhorn, *cor de chasse*,
corno di caccia, and "French" horn. Natural horns like this one were so called because they
could only produce the "natural" tones, that is, the incomplete scale which could be played on

the instrument before the addition of keys or valves. Such instruments were used until the beginning of the nineteenth century.

It was a fortunate inspiration of an unknown horn maker to adorn this instrument, which is made of clay, with gleaming faience in the beautiful blue and white Delft floral design.

New York, Metropolitan Museum of Art, 89.4.1115 (Crosby Brown Collection, 1889). Background: 48.187.695, silk-satin brocaded in gold, Italian, c. 1750 (bequest of Catharine D. Wentworth, 1948).

98 *Cornet in C with seven Bells*

Mid-19th century · Signed: "No 33329 Adolphe Sax 50 Rue St. Georges à Paris"

Sometimes the requirements of acoustics and the experimentations of an imaginative pioneer craftsman result in an instrument of new shape and, at the same time, irresistible appeal to the eye – though the latter may be only a by-product of the engineering.

The instrument illustrated here is in fact a combination of seven instruments of slightly different length, each with a separate tube and bell. The six valves control the way the air stream goes from the mouthpiece to one of the bells. If no valve is activated the air passes through a maximum length of tubing and leaves through the bell farthest away from the mouth-piece. If the first valve is set in action, the air stream is directed to the second bell, thus travelling a shorter distance, which results in a sound one half-tone lower; and so on.

The resulting design is of striking beauty. Out of the maze of tubing surrounding the two sets of pistons, the seven tubes emerge in a semicircular turn and, gradually widening, flare out in a cluster of seven oval bells – almost the surrealist abstraction of a multiheaded hydra, likely to receive a prize in any mid-twentieth-century exhibition of sculpture. The only drawback of this acoustically perfect construction is the great weight of the accumulation of tubes and valves and bells, a factor which may have prevented wide acceptance of the instrument.

Adolphe (actually Antoine Joseph) Sax was the son of the ingenious maker and inventor of wind instruments in Paris, Charles Joseph Sax, and was himself a celebrated pioneer in this field.

Brussels, Musée Instrumental of the Conservatoire (Catalogue by V. C. Mahillon, No. 2467).

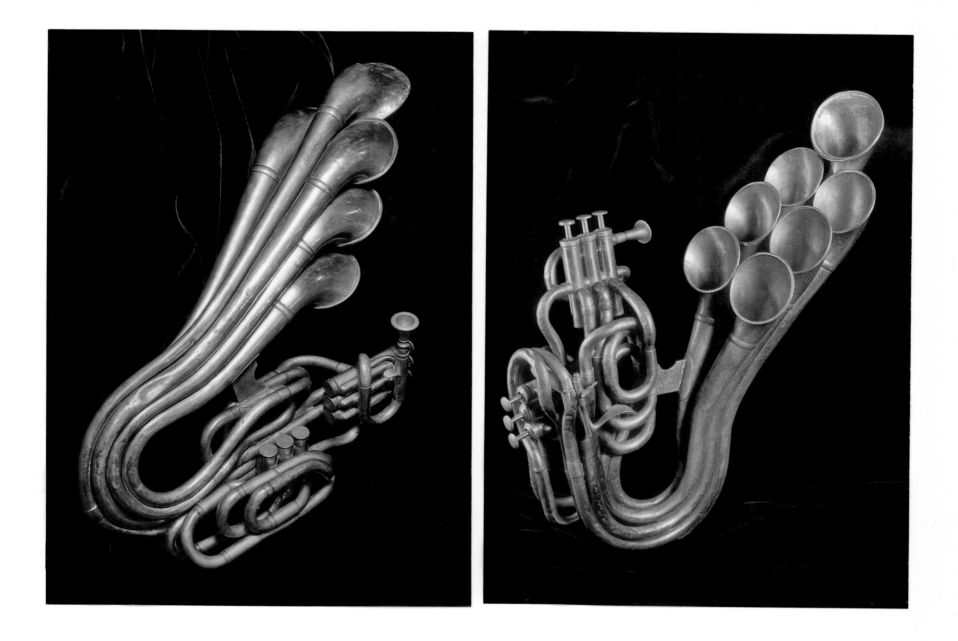

99 _Hand Horn in D (Cornet-Trompe)_
Belgian, early 19th century

Post Horn in B flat
Pelitti, Milan, early 19th century

Hunting Horn in D
Raoux, "Ordinair du Roy", Paris, c. 1760

The concert-goer, looking at the brass section of the modern orchestra, will find most of those instruments equipped with valves—additional sections of tube attached to the main tube, permitting the raising and lowering of pitch to obtain a complete chromatic scale. The player opens and closes these extra tubings by means of pistons or cylindrical devices which, together with the extra tubing, create the visual impression of a highly complex mechanism that is confusing to the eye.

This was not always so: valves are a relatively recent achievement in the history of brass instruments. They were invented in Germany in about 1815, and soon opened a completely new era in the making of brass instruments and, because of their practical merits, of orchestral music itself. Yet what the instruments gained in range and playing ease, they lost in eye appeal. The smooth, coiled tubes of horns were often of unparalleled beauty. Not even the invention of the additional U-shaped crooks during the eighteenth century, and of keys later on, could entirely destroy the elegance of this shape. A compact spiral of shining metal tube, expanding slowly at first and then rapidly into the flaring bell, is one of the instances where compliance with the immutable laws of acoustics, together with the demands of easy playability, resulted in a form of unsurpassed grace. No wonder that long after the invention of valves, some experimenters and instrument makers returned occasionally to the earlier form.
New York, Metropolitan Museum of Art, 89.4.1105, 89.4.2556, 89.4.2204 (Crosby Brown Collection, 1889).

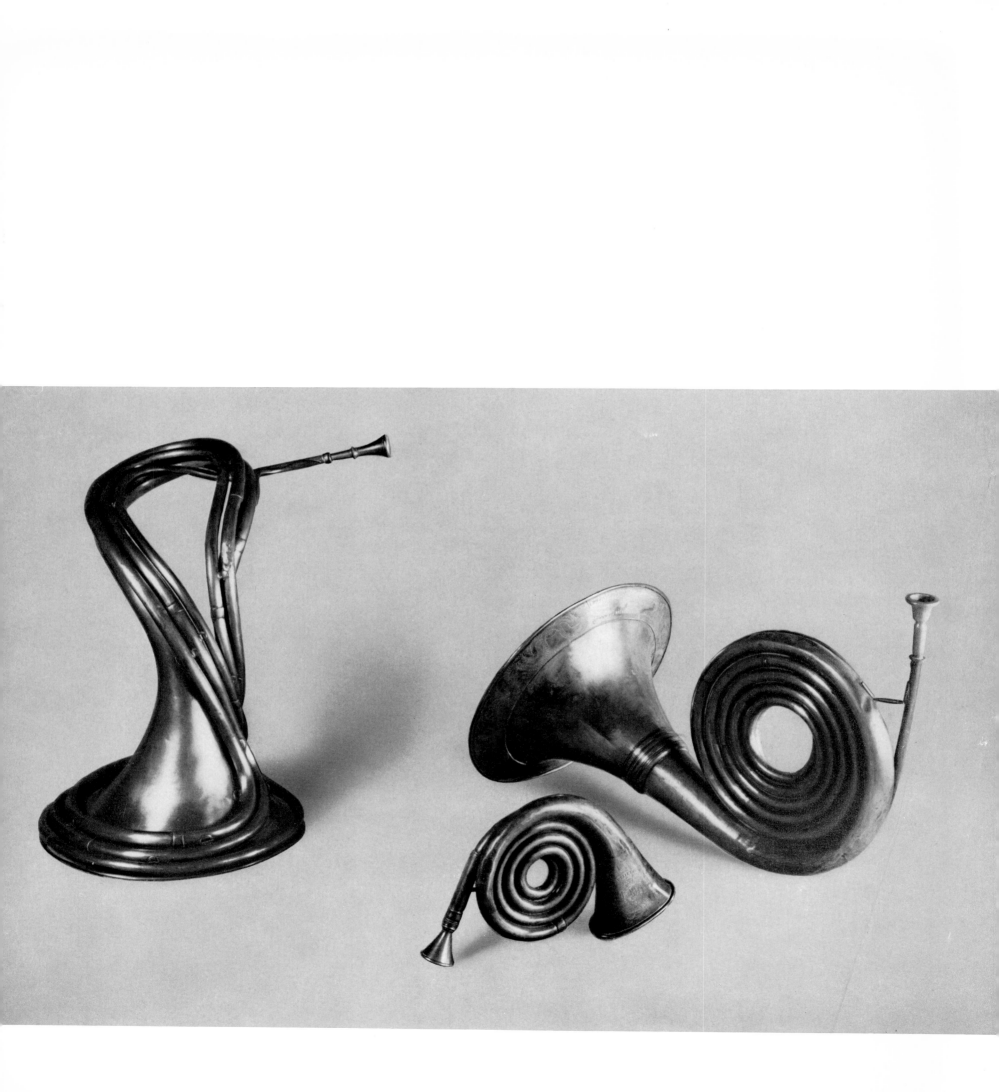

100 Grand Pianoforte

by Erard and Co., London, ca. 1840

Sébastien Érard (1752–1831) was the celebrated founder of the oldest and most famous piano manufactory of France. Son of a cabinet maker in Strassburg, he went to Paris in 1768. At first he built harpsichords, and then turned to pianoforte and harp construction, where he proved an outstanding pioneer, making many improvements and inventions for these instruments. His most radical and successful contribution to the pianoforte was in providing the action with double escapement ("double échappement") which made the "Piano d'Érard" world-famous. Beethoven owned an Érard piano from 1803 to 1816. Later, Érard instruments were favored by Hummel, Thalberg, Moscheler, Mendelssohn, Liszt, and Verdi. As early as 1786, Érard founded a branch of his firm in London. He died in 1831 in his castle, La Muette, near Paris, surrounded by his art collection.

The pianoforte shown here is not dated but was probably built around 1840. On it are the arms, monogram, and coronet of Thomas Henry, 4th Baron Foley, who was made a baron in 1833 and married in 1849 (when the coat of arms would have been changed to include that of his wife); the lock on the instrument indicates that it was made in the reign of Queen Victoria, who acceded to the throne of England in 1837. This pianoforte is the most lavishly decorated Érard piano, and probably has the most exquisite intarsias of any musical instrument ever made. The designer and executor of the case was an Englishman, George Henry Blake. The marquetry contains representations of grotesque animals, musical instruments and scenes, classical and antique statuary, floral designs, etc., in various woods, ivory, and mother-of-pearl inlays. Near to the coat of arms is a scene after one of the *Fêtes Venetiennes* of Watteau. Carved and gilded wood scrolls decorate the corners and edges of the case in floral, leaf, and shell designs, foliate motifs, and masks. A scrolling stretcher between the four legs has, at its center, a languid figure of Apollo resting on a lion mask; and the pedals are attached to a full-cheeked, grotesque mask with gilded birds perched on its head. The vast profusion of detail is, in the end, rendered homogeneous and beautiful to the beholder by the rich golden hue of the satin-wood case, which suffuses the whole instrument.

New York, Metropolitan Museum of Art, 59.76 (Gift of Mrs. Henry McSweeney, 1959).

FOOTNOTES

1 Cf. *Emanuel Winternitz*, The school of Gaudenzio Ferrari and the Early History of the Violin, in: The Commonwealth of Music, Writings on Music in History, Art, and Culture, in Honor of Curt Sachs, The Free Press, New York 1965.

2 Cf. *Emanuel Winternitz*, Bagpipes for the Lord, in: Metropolitan Museum of Art Bulletin, June 1958, p. 286.

3 Cf. *Alexander Hajdecki*, Die italienische Lira da Braccio: Eine kunsthistorische Studie zur Geschichte der Violine, Mostar (Herzegowina) 1892.

4 Cf. *Emanuel Winternitz*, Lira da Braccio, in: Die Musik in Geschichte und Gegenwart, vol. 8, Basel, London, New York 1960.

5 Cf. *Emanuel Winternitz*, Instruments de musique étranges chez Filippino Lippi, Piero di Cosimo et Lorenzo Costa, in: Les Fêtes de la Renaissance I, Editions du Centre National de la Recherche Scientifique, Paris 1956, p. 386.

6 Cf. *Emanuel Winternitz*, Leonardo's invention of the viola organista, in: Raccolta Vinciana, Fasc. XX, Mailand 1964.

7 For this information I wish to thank my colleague at the Metropolitan Museum of Art, Dr. Olga Raggio.

8 Cf. *Robert Enggass*, "La Musica Barberini del Lanfranco", in Commentarii, Anno X, no. 4, 1959.

9 Cf. *Emanuel Winternitz*, The Golden Harpsichord and Todini's Galleria Armonica, Metropolitan Museum Bulletin, vol. XIV, no. 5, 1956.

10 Cf. *Emanuel Winternitz*, The Survival of the Kithara and the Evolution of the English Cittern: A Study in Morphology, in: Journal of the Warburg and Courtauld Institutes, vol. XXIV, no. 3–4, London 1961.

11 Cf. *Emanuel Winternitz*, Bagpipes and hurdy-gurdies in their social setting, Metropolitan Museum Bulletin, New Series, vol. II, no. 1, 1943, p. 56 ff.

12 Cf. *Emanuel Winternitz*, Instruments de musique étranges chez Filippino Lippi, Piero di Cosimo et Lorenzo Costa, in: Les Fêtes de la Renaissance I, Editions du Centre National de la Recherche Scientifique, Paris 1956.

VIGNETTES

Page 222: Daniel Chodowiecki, "At the spinet", engraving.

Page 224: Daniel Chodowiecki, "Le Chant", engraving.

Page 230: "Marie Antoinette", engraving, 19th century.

Page 243: Johann Christoph Weigel, waldhorn player from "Musicalisches Theatrum", p. 7.

Page 246: "Courier", from the paper mill of Franz Depal Wurtz in Speyer, 1811.

Page 249: "Music Store", engraving, England, 19th century.

BIBLIOGRAPHY

GENERAL AND STANDARD WORKS

Armstrong, Robert Bruce. Musical Instruments: Pt. 1–The Irish and the Highland Harps, Edinburgh 1904; Pt. 2–English and Irish Instruments, 1908.

Bacher, Joseph. Die Viola da Gamba, Kassel 1932.

Bachmann, Werner. Die Anfänge des Streichinstrumentenspiels, Leipzig 1964.

Baines, Anthony. Bagpipes (Occasional Papers on Technology, 9, ed. by T. K. Penniman and B. M. Blackwood), Oxford 1960.

— Musical Instruments through the Ages, London 1961.

— Woodwind Instruments and their History, New York 1957.

Barton, Edwin Henry. A Text-Book on Sound, London 1926.

Bate, Philip. The Oboe, London 1956.

Berlioz, Hector. Grand traité d'instrumentation et d'orchestration modernes, Paris 1844.

Bessaraboff, Nicholas. Ancient European Musical Instruments: An Organological Study of the Musical Instruments in the Leslie Lindsey Mason Collection at the Museum of Fine Arts, Boston 1941.

Besseler, Heinrich. Die Musik des Mittelalters und der Renaissance, 10 parts, Wildpark-Potsdam 1931–1934.

Boalch, Donald H. Makers of the Harpsichord and Clavichord 1440 to 1840, London 1956.

Boehm, Theobald. Die Flöte und das Flötenspiel in akustischer, technischer und artistischer Beziehung, Munich 1871.

Boyden, David A. The History of Violin Playing from its Origins to 1761, London 1965.

Brencour, René. Histoire des instruments de musique... pref. by Ch. H. Widor, Paris 1921.

Bricqueville, Eugène de. Un coin de la curiosité. Les anciens instruments de musique, Paris 1895.

— Les musettes, Paris 1894.

— Notice sur la vielle, 2nd ed. Paris 1911.

— Les vents d'instruments de musique au XVIIIe siècle, Paris 1908.

— La viole d'amour, Paris 1908.

Broholm, H. C. and William P. Larsen and Godtfred Skjerne. The Lures of the Bronze Age, Copenhagen 1949.

Buchner, Alexander. Musical Instruments Through the Ages (trans. by Iris Urwin), London, n. d. (1952?).

Carse, Adam. Musical Wind Instruments: a History of the Wind Instruments used in European Orchestras and Wind-Bands from the Later Middle Ages to the Present Time, London 1939.

Daubeny, Ulric. Orchestral Wind Instruments, Ancient and Modern, London 1920.

Dolmetsch, Arnold. The Interpretation of the Music of the XVIIth and XVIIIth Centuries, London 1915.

— "The Lute", The Connoisseur, VIII, pp. 213–217 (April 1904); IX, pp. 23–28 (May 1904).

— "The Viols", The Connoisseur, X, pp. 134–138 (Nov. 1904); XIII, pp. 112–116 (Oct. 1905).

Dräger, Hans Heinz. Die Entwicklung des Streichbogens und seine Anwendung in Europa bis zum Violenbogen des 16. Jahrhunderts, Berlin, Kassel 1937.

Eichborn, Hermann. Die Trompete in alter und neuer Zeit, Leipzig 1881.

— Das alte Clarinblasen auf Trompeten, Leipzig 1894.

Ellerhorst, Winfred. Handbuch der Orgelkunde, Einsiedeln, Switzerland 1936.

Fétis, F. J. Antoine Stradivari, Luthier célèbre connu sous le nom de Stradivarius, Paris 1856.

Fryklund, Daniel. "Viola di Bardone", Svensk Tidskrift för Musikforskning IV (1922), pp. 129–152.

Galpin, Francis William. Old English Instruments of Music, their History and Character, 3rd ed. revised. London 1932.

— "The Sackbut, its Evolution und History", Proceedings of the Musical Association, XXXIII, 1906–1907 (Nov. 1906).

— A Textbook of European Musical Instruments, London 1937.

Goehlinger, Franz August. Geschichte des Klavichords, Basel 1910.

Grillet, Laurent. Les ancêtres du violon et du violoncello, les luthiers et les fabricants d'archets, 2 vols., Paris 1901, 1905.

Hajdecki, Alexander. Die italienische Lira da Braccio. Eine kunst-historische Studie zur Geschichte der Violine, Mostar (Herzogovina) 1892.

Harding, Rosamond E.M. The Piano-Forte, its History traced to the Great Exhibition of 1851, Cambridge 1933.

Harrison, Frank and Joan Rimmer. European Musical Instruments, London 1964.

Hart, George. The Violin: its Famous Makers and their Imitators, London 1875 (later eds. 1884, 1887, 1909).

Hayes, Gerald R. Musical Instruments and their Music, 1500–1750; Vol. 1–The Treatment of Instrumental Music, London 1928; Vol. 2–The Viols and other Bowed Instruments, London 1930.

Heron-Allen, Edward. Violin-Making, as it was and is: ...A Historical, Theoretical and Practical Treatise on the Science and Art of Violin Making... London 1884.

Hickman, Hans. Das Portativ, Kassel 1936.

Hill, William Henry and Arthur F. Hill and Alfred E. Hill. Antonio Stradivari, his Life and Work, London 1902, reprint (introd. by Sidney Beck), New York 1962.

— The Violin Makers of the Guarneri Family (1626–1762), London 1931.

Hornbostel, Erich H. von, and *Curt Sachs.* "Systematik der Musikinstrumente. Ein Versuch", Zeitschrift für Ethnologie, 1914, pp. 553–590.

Hubbard, Frank. Three Centuries of Harpsichord Making, Cambridge, Mass. 1965.

Jahn, Fritz. "Die Nürnberger Trompeten und Posaunenmacher im 16. Jahrhundert", Archiv für Musikwissenschaft, April 1926.

James, Philip. Early Keyboard Instruments from their Beginnungs to the Year 1820, London 1930, reprint 1960.

James, W. N. A Word or Two on the Flute, London 1836.

Kinkeldey, Otto. Orgel und Klavier in der Musik des 16. Jahrhunderts, Leipzig 1910.

Köhler, Werner Eginhard. Beiträge zur Geschichte und Literatur der Viola d'amore, Diss., Berlin 1938.

Körte, Oswald. Laute und Lautenmusik bis zur Mitte des 16. Jahrhunderts, Leipzig 1910.

Langwill, Lyndesay G. An Index of Musical Wind-Instrument Makers, 2nd and enlarged ed., Edinburgh 1962.

Lütgendorff, Willibald Leo, Freiherr von. Die Geigen- und Lautenmacher vom Mittelalter bis zur Gegenwart, 2 vols., Frankfurt am Main 1913.

Marcuse, Sibyl. Musical Instruments: a Comprehensive Dictionary, New York 1964.

Mauger, N. Les Hotteterre, Paris 1912.

Meer, J.H. van der. "Typologie der Sackpfeife", Anzeiger des Germanischen Nationalmuseums, Nürnberg 1964.

— "Zur Geschichte des Klaviziteriums", Bericht über den Internationalen Musikwissenschaftlichen Kongress Kassel 1962, Kassel–Basel–London–New York 1962.

Moreck, Kurt. Die Musik in der Malerei, Munich 1924.

Nef, Karl. Geschichte unserer Musikinstrumente, Leipzig 1926.

Norlind, Tobias. Systematik der Saiteninstrumente: I. Geschichte der Zither, Stockholm 1937.

Panum, Hortense. Middelalderens Strengeinstrumenter og deres Forløbere, 3 vols., Copenhagen 1915–1931.

Paul, Oscar. Geschichte des Claviers, Leipzig 1868.

Piersig, Fritz. Die Einführung des Hornes in die Kunstmusik..., Halle 1927.

Rendall, F. Geoffrey. The Clarinet, 2nd rev. ed., London 1957.

Rimbault, Edward F. The Pianoforte, its Origin, Progress, and Construction... London 1860.

Rockstro, Richard S. A Treatise on the Construction, the History, and the Practice of the Flute... London 1890, revised ed. 1928.

Rupp, Emile. Die Entwicklungsgeschichte der Orgelbaukunst, Einsiedeln 1929.

Russell, Raymond. The Harpsichord and Clavichord, London 1959.

Sachs, Curt. Geist und Werden der Musikinstrumente, Berlin 1929.

— Handbuch der Musikinstrumentenkunde, Leipzig 1920, 2nd ed. 1930.

— The History of Musical Instruments, New York 1940.

— Das Klavier, Berlin 1923.

— Musik und Oper am kurbrandenburgischen Hof, Berlin 1910.

— Real-Lexikon der Musikinstrumente, zugleich ein Polyglossar für das gesamte Instrumentengebiet, Berlin 1913; reprint 1962; 2nd rev. enlarged ed., New York 1964.

— The Rise of Music in the Ancient World, New York 1943.

— "La signification, la tâche et la technique muséographique des collections d'instruments de musique", Mouseion, XIII, nos. III-IV, pp. 153–184 (1934).

Saint-George, Henry, The Bow, 3rd ed., London 1922.

Schaeffner, André. Origine des instruments de musique, Paris 1936.

— "Projet d'une classification nouvelle des instruments de musique", Bulletin du Musée d'Ethnologie du Trocadéro, no. 1 (1931), pp. 21–25.

— "D'une nouvelle classification méthodique des instruments de musique", Revue Musicale 1932, pp. 215–231.

Schlesinger, Kathleen. The Instruments of the Modern Orchestra & Early Records of the Precursors of the Violin Family, 2 vols., London 1910.

Straeten, Edmund van der. The History of the Violin: its Ancestors and Collateral Instruments, from Earliest Times to the Present Day, 2 vols., London and Toronto 1933.

— The History of the Violoncello, the Viol da Gamba, their Precursors... London 1915.

Terry, Charles Sanford. Bach's Orchestra, London 1932.

Vidal, Louis Antoine. Les instruments à archet..., 3 vols., Paris 1876.

Viollet-le-Duc. Dictionnaire raisonné du mobilier français de l'epoque carlovingienne à la renaissance, Paris 1858–1875. 6 vols. "Instruments de musique", vol. II, pt. 4, pp. 243–327.

Wasielewski, Wilhelm Joseph von. Die Violine im XVII. Jahrhundert und die Anfänge der Instrumentalcomposition, Bonn 1874.

— Die Violine und ihre Meister, 5th ed. (Waldemar von Wasielewski, ed.), Leipzig 1910.

— The Violoncello and its History (Isobella S. E. Stigand, tr.), London 1894.

Welch, Christopher, History of the Boehm Flute, London 1885. 3rd ed. 1896.

— Six Lectures on the Recorder and other Flutes, London 1911.

Welcker von Gontershausen, Heinrich. Neu eröffnetes Magazin musikalischer Tonwerkzeuge..., Frankfurt am Main 1855.

Winternitz, Emanuel. "Bagpipes and Hurdy-Gurdies in their Social Setting", Metropolitan Museum of Art Bulletin, Summer 1943.

— "The Early History of the Organ", for Columbia Records, THE ORGAN (Columbia Masterworks DL 5288), September 1958.

— "The Evolution of the Baroque Orchestra", Metropolitan Museum of Art Bulletin, May 1954.

— Keyboard Instruments in the Metropolitan Museum of Art, New York 1961.

— "Lira da Braccio", Die Musik in Geschichte und Gegenwart, Vol. 8, col. 935–954, Basel–Kassel–London–New York 1960.

— "On Archlutes", Guitar Review, No. 9, 1949.

— "The School of Gaudenzio Ferrari and the Early History of the Violin", The Commonwealth of Music... writings in honor of Curt Sachs, Gustave Reese and Rose Brandel, eds., New York 1965.

— "The Survival of the Kithara and the Evolution of the English Cittern: A Study in Morphology", Journal of the Warburg and Courtauld Institutes, Vol. XXIV, Nos. 3–4, London 1961.

Zingel, Hans Joachim, Harfe und Harfenspiel, Halle 1932.

TREATISES BEFORE 1800

Utrecht Psalter. Autotype facsimile; published by the Palaeographical Society, London 1875. Miniature representations of musicians and musical instruments adorn this volume originally made in the 9th century.

Cantigas de Santa Maria. A collection of tunes and miniature representations of musicians and instruments made for Alfonso X ("El Sabio"), king of Castile and León, 1252–1284.

Die Manessesche Liederhandschrift. Faksimile-Ausgabe, introductions by Rudolf Sillib, Friedrich Panzer, Arthur Haseloff, Leipzig 1924–1927. Many plates have representations of musical instruments in this book which first appeared in the 14th century.

Bartolomeo Ramos de Pareja. De Musica Tractatus, sive Musica Practica..., Bononias 1482.

Franchino Gafori. Practica musice..., 1496.

Arnold Schlick. Spiegel der Orgelmacher und Organisten, Heidelberg 1511.

Sebastian Virdung. Musica getutscht und ausgezogen durch Sebastianum Virdung Priesters von Amberg..., Basel 1511 (facsimile ed., Robert Eitner, ed., Berlin 1882).

Franchino Gafori. ...De Harmonia Musicorum Instrumentorum Opus, Milan 1518.

Hans Judenkunig. Utilis et compendiaria introductio, Vienna 1523.

Martin Agricola. Musica Instrumentalis Deudsch..., Wittemberg 1528 and 1545 (reprint, Leipzig 1896).

Hans Gerle. Musica Teusch auf die Instrument die Grossen und kleynen Geigen auch Lautten..., Nürnberg 1532 (2nd ed. 1546).

Giovanni Maria Lanfranco. Scintille di musica, Brescia 1533.

Silvestro Canassi dal Fontego. Opera intitulata Fontegara, Venice 1535 (modern reprint in Collezione di Trattati e Musiche Antiche Edite in Facsimile, Milan 1934).

— Regola Rubertina: Vol. 1 – Regola che insegna a sonare de Viola d'arco tastada, Venice 1542; Vol. 2 – Lettione seconda pur della prattica di sonare il Violone d'arco da tasti, 1543 (modern reprint Max Schneider, ed., Leipzig 1924).

Henricus Glareanus. Δωδε Κάχοςδον, Basel 1547.

Diego Ortiz. Tratado de glosas, Rome 1553.

Juan Bermudo. Declaracion de instrumentos musicales, Ossuna 1555.

Massimo Trojano. Discorsi, Monaco 1568.

Vincenzo Galilei. Dialogo... della musica antica, et della moderna, Florence 1581 (2nd ed. 1602).

Lodovico Zacconi. Prattica di musica... divisa in quattro libri, Venice 1596.

Giulio Caccini. La nuova musiche, Florence 1601 (reprint, Francesco Vatielli, ed., Rome 1934).

Scipione Cerreto. Della prattica musica vocale et strumentale..., Naples 1609.

Pedro Cerone. El melopeo y maestro, Naples 1613.

Michael Praetorius. Syntagma Musicum, Wittemberg and Wolfenbüttel 1615–1620 (reprints: Berlin 1884 and Kassel 1929).

Marin Mersenne. Harmonie universelle..., 2 vols., Paris 1636–1637.

Athanasius Kircher. Musurgia Universalis..., 2 vols., Rome 1650.

John Playford. A Breefe Introduction to the Skill or Musick, for Song & Violl, London 1654 (1st ed.; other editions with various subtitles, 1658–1697).

Thomas Mace. Musick's Monument, London 1676.

Jean Rousseau. Traité de le viole, Paris 1687.

Johann Mattheson. Das neu-eröffnete Orchestre, Hamburg 1713.

Filippo Buonanni. Gabineto armonico pieno d'istromanti sonori indicati..., Rome 1722.

Ernst Gottlieb Baron. Historisch-theoretische und praktische Untersuchung der Lauten, Nürnberg 1727.

Denis Diderot and Jean Lorond d'Alembert, eds. Encyclopédie, 17 vols., Paris/ Neuchâtel 1751–1765.

Johann Joachim Quantz. Versuch einer Anweisung die Flöte traversiere zu spielen, Berlin 1752 (Breslau 1780, 1789).

Karl Philipp Emanuel Bach. Versuch über die wahre Art das Clavier zu spielen, Berlin 1753.

Leopold Mozart. Versuch einer gründlichen Violinschule, Augsburg 1756 (reprint, Vienna 1922).

Jacob Adlung. Musica mechanica organoedi..., Johann Lorenz Albrecht, ed., 2 vols., Berlin 1768.

François Bedos de Celles. L'Art du facteur d'orgues, 2 vols., Paris 1776–1778 (reprint, Kassel 1934).

Johann Ernst Altenburg. Versuch einer Anleitung zur heroisch-musikalischen Trompeter- und Pauker-Kunst, Halle 1795 (reprint, Leipzig 1911).

HISTORY OF COLLECTING

Anglés, H. "La musica en la Corte de Carlos V", Monumentos de la Música Española, II, Barcelona 1944.

Berner, Alfred. "Instrumentensammlungen", Die Musik in Geschichte und Gegenwart, Basel-London 1957, Vol. 6, col. 1295–1510. (A comprehensive list of collections of musical instruments and catalogues of such collections.)

Borghini, Raffaello. Il Riposo, Florence 1584.

Bricqueville, Eugène de. "Les collections d'instruments de musique aux XVIe, XVIIe et XVIIIe siècles", Un coin de la curiosité. Les anciens instruments de musique, Paris 1895.

Burckhardt, Jakob. "Die Sammler", Beiträge zur Kunstgeschichte von Italien, Basel 1898.

Galpin, F. W. Old English Instruments of Music, London 1910, 1932.

Kinsky, Georg. "Musikinstrumenten-Sammlung in Vergangenheit und Gegenwart", Jahrbuch der Musikbibliothek Peters, 1921. Vol. 27, pp. 47–60.

Langwill, L. G. "Instruments, Collections of", Grove's Dictionary of Music and Musicians, 5th ed., New York 1955, Vol. IV, pp. 509–515.

Müntz, Eugène. Les Collections des Médicis, Paris 1888.

Parigi, Luigi. Laurentiana, Florence 1954.

Pedrell, F. Emporio científico e histórico de Organografía musical antigua española, Barcelona 1901.

Puliti, L. "Cenni storici della vita del Serenissimo Ferdinando dei Medici Granprincipe di Toscana e della origine del pianoforte", Atti dell'Accademia del Regio Istituto Musicale di Firenze, 1874.

Sachs, Curt. Musik und Oper am kurbrandenburgischen Hofe, Berlin 1910.

Sandberger, Adolf. "Bemerkungen zur Biographie Hans Leo Hasslers...", Denkmäler Deutscher Tonkunst in Bayern V/1, Leipzig 1904. (It concerne the Fugger collection, Augsburg.)

Sansovino, Francesco. Venezia descritta, 1581.

Stockbauer, Jacob. "Kunstbestrebungen am bayrischen Hofe", Quellenschriften für Kunstgeschichte, Vol. 8, Vienna 1874.

Straeten, Edmond van der. La Musique aux Pays-Bas, vol. 1–8, Brussels 1867–1888.

Winternitz, Emanuel. "The Golden Harpsichord and Todini's Galleria Armonica", Metropolitan Museum of Art Bulletin, February 1956. (It concerns the collection of Michele Todini in Rome in the 17th century.)

CATALOGUES OF COLLECTIONS

Bayerisches Nationalmuseum, Munich. Ausstellung alter Musikinstrumente; Noten und Dokumente aus drei Jahrhunderten (November-December 1951), Munich 1951.

Cervelli, Luisa. "Mostra di Antichi Strumenti Musicali"; a catalogue of the 1963/64 exhibition Teatro Comunale, Modena, which included instruments from the Museo Civico di Modena and the Museo Civico di Bologna, Modena 1963.

Chouquot, Gustave. Le Musée du Conservatoire National de Musique: catalogue descriptif et raisonné (with 3 supplements by Léon Pillaut), Paris 1875 and 1884, 1894, 1899, 1903.

Claudius Collection, Copenhagen. Carl Claudius' Samling af Gamle Musikinstrumenter, Copenhagen 1931.

Dart, Thurston. "The Instruments in the Ashmolean Museum", Galpin Society Journal, no. 7, 1954.

Densmore, Frances. Handbook of the Collection of Musical Instruments in the United States National Museum, Bulletin 136, Washington 1927.

Engel, Carl. A Descriptive Catalogue of the Musical Instruments in the South Kensington Museum, London 1870 (2nd ed., 1874).

Hammerich, Angul. Das Musikhistorische Museum zu Kopenhagen: beschreibender Katalog, Copenhagen 1911.

Hipkins, Alfred James. A Description and History of the Pianoforte and of the Older Keyboard Stringed Instruments, London 1896.

Kinsky, Georg. Kleiner Katalog der Sammlung alter Musikinstrumente, Köln 1913.

— Musikhistorisches Museum von Wilhelm Heyer in Köln: Katalog, 2 vols. Köln 1910, 1912.

Mahillon, Victor Charles. Catalogue descriptif et analytique du Musée Instrumental du Conservatoire Royal de Musique de Bruxelles, 2nd ed., 5 vols., Ghent 1893–1922.

Mandyczewski, Eusebius. Inventory of the Museum of the Gesellschaft der Musikfreunde in Vienna, in the Zusatz-Band zur Geschichte der k. k. Gesellschaft der Musikfreunde in Wien, Vienna 1912.

Marcuse, Sibyl. Musical Instruments at Yale; catalogue of the exhibition at the Yale University Art Gallery, February-March 1960.

Metropolitan Museum of Art, New York. Catalogue of the Crosby Brown Collection of Musical Instruments of All Nations, 6 vols., New York 1903–1914.

Miller, Dayton C. Catalogue of Books and Literary Material Relating to the Flute and other Musical Instruments, Cleveland 1935.

Museum of Fine Arts, Boston. "The Leslie Lindsey Mason Collection of Musical Instruments", The Museum of Fine Arts Bulletin, no. 91, Boston 1917.

Rubardt, Paul. Führer durch das Musikinstrumenten-Museum der Karl-Marx-Universität Leipzig, Leipzig 1964.

Sachs, Curt. Sammlung alter Musikinstrumente bei der staatlichen Hochschule für Musik zu Berlin: beschreibender Katalog, Berlin 1913.

Schlosser, Julius, Ritter von. Die Sammlung alter Musikinstrumente, Kunsthistorisches Museum in Wien, Vienna 1920.

Skinner, William. The Belle Skinner Collection of Old Musical Instruments, Holyoke, Massachusetts (Fanny Reed Hammond and Nils J. Ericsson, compilers), Holyoke, Mass., 1933.

Stanley, Albert A. Catalogue of the Stearns Collection of Musical Instruments, New York 1916, new ed. 1928.

Wit, Paul de. Katalog des musikhistorischen Museums von Paul de Wit, Leipzig, Leipzig 1903.

MUSICAL INSTRUMENTS IN THE VISUAL ARTS:

Bernardi, Marziano, and *Andrea della Corte.* "Gli strumenti musicali nei dipinti della Galleria degli Uffizi", Edizioni Radio Italiana, Turin 1952.

Buhle, Edward. Die musikalischen Instrumente in den Miniaturen des frühen Mittelalters, Leipzig 1903.

Kinsky, Georg. Gesichte der Musik in Bildern, Leipzig 1929.

Marcucci, Luisa. "Mostra di strumenti musicali in disegni degli Uffizi", Olschki, Florence 1952.

Parigi, Luigi. "I disegni musicali del Gabinetto degli Uffizi", Olschki, Florence 1951.

Pincherle, Marc. An Illustrated History of Music (trans. by Rollo Myers), New York 1959.

Rorimer, James J. "A Double-virginal dated 1581 by Hans Ruckers", Metropolitan Museum Studies, vol. 2, 1929–1930, pp. 176–186.

Sauerlandt, Max. Die Musik in fünf Jahrhunderten der Europäischen Malerei, Leipzig, 1922.

Winternitz, Emanuel. "Archeologia musicale del rinascimento nel Parnaso di Raffaello", Rendiconti della Pontificia Accademia Romana di Archeologia, Vol. XXVII 1952–1954.

— "Bagpipes for the Lord", Metropolitan Museum of Art Bulletin, June 1958.

— "Instruments de Musique étranges chez Filippino Lippi, Piero di Cosimo et Lorenzo Costa", Les Fêtes de la Renaissance, I, Editions du Centre National de la Recherche Scientifique, Paris 1956.

— "A Lira da Braccio in Giovanni Bellini's »Feast of the Gods«", Art Bulletin, Vol. XXVIII, no. 2, June 1946.

— "Muses and Music in a Burial Chapel: An Interpretation of Filippino Lippi's Window Wall in the Cappella Strozzi", Mitteilungen des kunsthistorischen Institutes in Florenz, Band XI, Heft 4, September 1965.

— "Musicians and Musical Instruments in »The Hours of Charles the Noble«", The Bulletin of the Cleveland Museum of Art, Vol. 52, No. 3, March 1965.

— "Quattrocento Science in the Gubbio Study", Metropolitan Museum of Art Bulletin, October 1942.

— "Quattrocento-Intarsien als Quellen der Instrumentengeschichte", Bericht über den siebenten Internationalen Musikwissenschaftlichen Kongress, Köln 1958.

— "The Visual Arts as a Source for the Historian of Music", International Musicological Society Congress Report, New York 1961.

INDEX

WAnn man die Warheit sagen will/
Sol ist die Geig das ältest Spil/
Welchs Zubal vor der Sündflut fand
Deß sich darnach auch vnterwand

Apollo/ für ein Gott gehalten:
Vnd schreiben doch dabei die Alten
Das im die Geigen geben hab
Mercurius/ für ein Heroldostab/

Die hat drei Seyten vberauß
Gspannt vber ein Merschneckenhauß:
Vil Instrument von ir entspringen:
Drum libt man sie vor allen dinge. 2

HOmerus zweiffelt billich wol
Ob man von Menschen glauben soll
Daß sie die Laut erfunden haben/
Oder ob sie die Götter gaben: .

Weils die größt Kunst ist/ schönster thon/
Vnd aller Instrument ein Kron/
Vnd hat was himlisch lieblichkeit:
Drum schreibt er sie sei zubereit

Vom Mercurio/ der dieselb
Hat rund dem Himel gleich gewelbt:
Auff das sie auch recht hümlisch laut:
Ke.n schönerer Bau ward nie erbaut.

GAr manche Pfeiff erfand der Pan/
Von dem nichts häßlichs komen kan/
Weil er soll sein der Bauren Gott/
Der hat zusamen auch gerott

Die Rußpfeiff/ Schalmen/ wie man meint/
Die Sackpfeiff seyn in auch verfreunt:
Welch man zwar muß lan passieren:
Das der Musick Namen füren:

Dann so die Musick ist vmb freud
Erdacht/ vnd vmb ergehlichkeit/
So muß man die nit schlecht verlachen/
Die weil sie auch vil kurtzweil machen. 9

DIe schön Spartanisch Policei/
Wie sie groß Krig fürt mancherlei/
Da hat sie gantz wol bedacht/
Die Zinkenhörner auffgepracht:

Das man sie prauch zu Feld im Hör/
Auf das sie machten ghertzer mehr/
Damit zu geben auch ein zeichen
Wa man vom Feind hin solte weichen/

Vnd in was schütten/ gang/ vnd lauf
An Feind solt gahn der gantze Hauf:
Heut aber seunds im Krig abkomen/
Man praucht dafür Trometl Trome. 7